Granger Index

✿ ✿ ✿ ✿ ✿ ✿ ✿ ✿ ✿ ✿

GRACE MARIE STANISTREET'S RECITATIONS FOR CHILDREN

Grace Marie Stanistreet

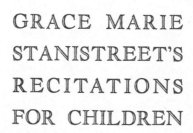

GRACE MARIE STANISTREET'S RECITATIONS FOR CHILDREN

GRANGER BOOK CO., INC.
Great Neck, N.Y.

First Published 1930
Reprinted 1978

International Standard Book Number 0-89609-076-0

PRINTED IN THE UNITED STATES OF AMERICA

✿ ✿ ✿ ✿ ✿ ✿ ✿ ✿ ✿ ✿

Affectionately Dedicated

To The Lower School

OF

The National School of Elocution and Oratory

Foreword

THE problem of material is one of the biggest difficulties the teacher of expression has to meet. This book of recitations for young people is sent forth in the hope that it will prove a partial solution to the familiar query — "What shall we say."

GRACE MARIE STANISTREET

Acknowledgments

THE editor wishes to thank the poets whose work has made this volume possible and make acknowledgment to the publishers who hold the copyrights hereby recorded.

The Parent's Magazine — for Mammy's Treasuh by Alice Drake.

American Poetry Magazine — for Point of View by Hazel Harper Harris.

The Spectator — for The Awakening by Patrick Chalmer and The Fly In Church by Jocelyn C. Lea.

The Commonweal — for The Song of A Smiling Lady by Katherine Bregy.

The Delineator — for Next Door Dog by Dixie Willson.

Doubleday Doran and Co. — for A Christmas Present for A Lady from Little Citizens by Myra Kelley.

The Macmillan Co. — for Thanksgiving from The Child On His Knees by Mary Dixon Thayer.

Harper and Brothers — for The Rag Dolly's Valentine from The Laughing Muse by Arthur Guiterman.

The Christian Science Monitor — for The Child's Dream by Isabel Fiske Conant and My Nursery Walls by Aileen Beaufort.

Child Life — for Pierrot, and The Two Little Shadows by Mildred Plew Merryman.

Reilly and Lee Co. — for Practicing Time by Edgar Guest from the book Rhymes of Childhood, copyright 1924 by the Reilly and Lee Co.   Reprinted by special permission.

Oneka Firefly — for Gratitude by Polly Hunter, Celestial Food by Cecelia Slawik Lamb, and Grievous Words by Suzanne Lehman.

The editor also wishes to acknowledge the efforts of Miss Betty Solliday in preparing this book for publication, and the many friends who have aided in various ways.

CONTENTS

POEMS FOR KINDERGARTEN AND PRIMARY GRADES

POEMS FOR INTERMEDIATE GRADES

[14]

POEMS FOR HIGH SCHOOL STUDENTS

PROSE FOR READING AND RECITATION

POEMS FOR HOLIDAY OCCASIONS

POEMS TO COSTUME

POEMS FOR KINDERGARTNERS
AND
PRIMARY GRADES

Pippa's Song

THE year's at the spring,
And day's at the morn;
Morning's at seven;
The hillside's dew-pearled:
The lark's on the wing;
The snail's on the thorn;
God's in his heaven —
All's right with the world!

ROBERT BROWNING

Recitations for Children

❋ ❋ ❋

ACTIONS SPEAK LOUDER

(*A doll to a little girl*)

I hug each little thing you do close to my heart;
I'm loving you, just loving you, but mine's the quiet part.
So many people talk too much that silence is an art.

And so I hold my tongue and let the precious moments fly;
My throat grows tight, my lips are set — do you ever wonder
    why?
Because I love you far too much to have speech satisfy!

PETER A. LEA

❖ ❖ ❖

MOTHER LOVE

(*A little girl to her doll*)

Your face is all washed off, dear,
   'Cause you's left out in the rain
An' you hasn't any mouf to kiss,
   But I'll kiss you just the same.
You can't cry — poor Dolly —
   'Cause you hasn't any eyes,
But I love you twice as much, dear
   Now you look so sad and wise.

GRACE DRAYTON

BETTY'S SONG TO HER DOLL

Matilda Jane, you never look
At any toy or picture book!
I show you pretty things in vain —
You must be blind, Matilda Jane!

I ask you riddles, tell you tales,
But all our conversation fails.
You never answer me again —
I fear you're dumb, Matilda Jane!

Matilda darling, when I call
You never seem to hear at all —
I shout with all my might and main —
But you're so deaf, Matilda Jane!

Matilda Jane, you needn't mind,
For though you're deaf and dumb and blind,
There's someone loves you, it is plain —
And that is me, Matilda Jane!

LEWIS CARROLL

GRANDMOTHER'S POLLY

When I was small I used to go
To Grandma's in summer to stay.
I loved next to Grandma, Polly,
The doll she kept for children's play.

Now Polly was a homey doll
All soft and floppy, 'cept her head.
The face I knew was her second,
It wasn't much for looks; instead

Her eyes were understanding blue.
You could tell by the way she flopped
How very dearly she loved you.
It hurts to think how she's been dropped.

Her head was hard as I have said,
But soft was the heart of Polly,
I know — though unbelievers scoff —
But they never loved a Dolly.

In heaven I won't ask about wings or crowns
Should they overlook my folly,
I'll say to him who lets deservers in,
" Please, Peter, where is Polly? "

GRACE MARIE STANISTREET

❖   ❖   ❖

THE THINKER DOG

Some foolish grown-ups say that dogs don't think.
I had a little dog, his nose, by some mistake, was pink,
But all his licky tongue
Was black as ink.
  He was a chow
  And that was how
His tongue was black as ink.

If I should get my hat
And never speak to him at all
He'd go lie in the hall
And look, oh my, how sad.

But if I even gave a wink
He'd jump and dance and make high-jink
And be as glad as glad.

Now tell me, why should he lie down
Did I but frown,
And then cavort and make high-jink
Did I but wink, —
If puppy-dogs don't think?

MARY A. HIPPLE

❖ ❖ ❖

BUTTER AND SOMETHING

I went to the store
To buy butter and something.
I bought the butter, but
The something I forgot.
"Was it crackers?" said the storeman,
"Was it eggs — was it pickles?"
But I knew it wasn't crackers,
And pickles it was not.
"Was it lemons?" asked a lady,
A funny old lady —
"Or maybe it was beans
That you serve in a pot?"
But I don't like lemons;
The beans were cold and shiny,
So I knew it wasn't beans
'Cause we eat our beans hot.
A little girl with curls said,
"Boy, was it cookies,
Little chocolate cookies

With a nut like a dot?"
And I said, " Why, yes, 'twas cookies —
Oh, I'm sure it must be cookies."
So I told the store man " Cookies,"
And I went home with a lot.

❖ ❖ ❖

MY CHILD

(*To " Sister "*)

Dolly and I were the best of good friends
And we had just wonderful times,
But though I helped her ever so much
She just wouldn't say my nursery rhymes.

I'd tell her over and over again
About Mary and her lamb,
And that awful child wouldn't say a word,
Just to be naughty — for I know she can.

Then I got provoked and told my Mama
And she said that Dolly was young.
But I've had her two months
And there's no excuse if her brain hasn't yet begun.

I had a long talk with my child today
And I've put her away for awhile.
I simply can't play with a baby you see —
'Cause I'm a grown-up child.

CAROL FLORENCE DERBY

CHILD TO A ROSE

White Rose, talk to me;
  I don't know what to do.
Why do you say no word to me,
  Who says so much to you?
I'm bringing you a little rain,
  And I shall be so proud,
If, when you feel it on your face,
  You take me for a cloud.
Here I come so softly,
  You cannot hear me walking;
If I take you by surprise,
  I may catch you talking.

White Rose, are you tired
  Of staying in one place?
Do you ever wish to see
  The wild flowers face to face?
Do you know the woodbines,
  And the big brown-crested reeds?
Do you wonder how they live
  So friendly with the weeds?
Have you any work to do
  When you've finished growing?
Shall you teach your little buds
  Pretty ways of blowing?

Do you ever go to sleep?
  Once I woke by night
And looked out of the window,
  And there you stood moon-white,—
Moon-white in a mist of darkness,—
  With never a word to say;
But you seemed to move a little,
  And then I ran away.

I should have felt no wonder
  After I hid my head,
If I had found you standing
  Moon-white beside my bed.

White Rose, do you love me?
  I only wish you'd say.
I would work hard to please you,
  If I but knew the way.
It seems so hard to be loving,
  And not a sign to see
But the silence and the sweetness
  For all as well as me.
I think you nearly perfect,
  In spite of all your scorns;
But, White Rose, if I were you,
  I wouldn't have those thorns.

❖ ❖ ❖

THE DEATH OF COCK ROBIN AND JENNY WREN

'Twas a cold autumn morning when Jenny Wren died,
  Cock Robin sat by for to see.
And when all was over he bitterly cried,
  So kind and so loving was he.

He buried her under the little moss heap
  That lies at the foot of the yew,
And by day and by night he sat near her to weep,
  Till his feathers were wet with the dew.

"Oh, Jenny, I am tired of lingering here,
  Through the dreary dark days of November,
And I'm thinking of nothing but you, Jenny dear,
  And our loving fond ways I remember.

"I think how you looked in your little brown suit,
  When you said that you'd always be mine;
With your fan in your hand, how you glanced at the fruit,
  And said you liked cherries and wine!

"I think of the sweet merry days of the spring,
  Of the nest that we built both together,
Of the dear little brood nestled under your wing,
  And the joys of the warm summer weather."

And as he lamented, the rain did down pour
  Till his body was wet through and through;
And he sang, "Dearest Jenny, my sorrows are o'er,
  And I'm coming, my true love, to you."

So he gathered some brown leaves to lay by her side,
  And to pillow his poor weary head,
And sang, "Jenny, my lost one, my fond one, my bride,"
  Till the gallant Cock Robin fell dead.

GERDA FAY

❖   ❖   ❖

Eddy and Davy have teeth and teeth
So they need teethbrushes right now;
But dear little Edith just eat'th and eat'th
The juice of the nice moo-ly cow.

Now Eddy and Davy have bunnies for bibs,
And bibs for their very good chow;
While dear little Edith still eat'th and eat'th
The juice of the nice moo-ly cow.

But dear little Edith is growing up fast,
She'll soon be promoted to chow;
And then *she* will need a pink bunny for bib
And *cream* from a *very* nice cow.

The first thing y' know she'll have teeth and teeth,
As Eddy and Davy do now,
Then she too shall have a nice teethbrush for teeth
That chew porridge and cream of de cow.

Oh, Eddy and Davy have teeth and teeth
So they need teethbrushes right now;
But dear little Edith still eat'th and eat'th
The juice of the nice moo-ly cow!

ANN BUDDY

❖ ❖ ❖

THE ORPHAN MOON

I often lie awake and see
The moon go sailing through the sky
Alone! Poor man, if that was me
I know I'd just get scared an' cry.
He does too, 'cause the other night
When mother tucked me safe in bed
I looked, but he was not in sight.
Then I knew he'd covered his head
An' was cryin' 'cause his great big tears
Came splash! splash! on my window sill
Like any little boy who fears
The dark and lonely night until
His mother takes him in her arms
An' sings one song an' then another —
Away all ugly things she charms,
Poor Moon! I don't believe he's got a mother!

LAURA HEEBNER BESTER

[29]

THE NEW MOON

Dear Mother, how pretty
The moon looks tonight!
She was never so lovely before;
The two little horns
Are so sharp and so bright,
I hope she'll not grow any more.

If I were up there,
With you and my friends,
I'd swing in it nicely, you'd see;
I'd sit in the middle
And hold by both ends;
Oh, what a bright swing it would be!

I would call to the stars
To keep out of the way,
Lest we should rock over their toes;
And then I would swing
Till the dawn of the day,
And see where the pretty moon goes.

And here we would stay
In the beautiful skies,
And through the bright clouds we would roam;
We would see the sun set,
And see the sun rise,
And on the next rainbow come home.

MRS. FOLLEN

MOONOLOGUE

Look at that moon up there winking at me;
He's caught in a cloud and just half of him's free.
He winked and I frowned and now all of him's hid!
Come out, Mr. Moon, I'm not cross if I did
Look that way. I'm just sad 'cause you're bound,
And that was a sad little frown that I frowned.
Come out again please, and I'll look pleasant too.
Hello, Mr. Moon, see me smiling at you?

KATHRYN REINHARD

❖ ❖ ❖

FAIRIES' SONG

We the fairies blithe and antic,
Of dimensions not gigantic,
Though the moonshine mostly keep us
Oft in orchards frisk and peep us.

Stolen sweets are always sweeter;
Stolen kisses much completer;
Stolen looks are nice in chapels;
Stolen, stolen be your apples.

When to bed the world is bobbing,
Then's the time for orchard-robbing;
Yet the fruit were scarce worth peeling
Were it not for stealing, stealing.

THOMAS DEQUINCEY

FLOATING CLOUD

I saw a cloud go sailing by,
It really was up very high,
And pretty, too.

It looked as if it most could float
As good as any little boat,
And lightly, too.

I looked again my cloud to see,
But it had gone away from me,
And quickly, too.

MARIANNE J. CORNELL

❖ ❖ ❖

FLOWERS

What is so beautiful as a flower?
Flowers whose petals are golden yellow,
Flowers that wash their faces in sunshine,
Flowers whose fragrance is soft and mellow.

Flowers whose hearts are store-rooms for bees,
Sweet smelling incense for children at play;
Flowers that are plucked for their beauty and odor,
Flowers that live in the sunshine each day.

ANNA B. COUGHLIN (12 years)

❖ ❖ ❖

A LITTLE BOY'S TALK WITH GOD

Dear God, I'm awful tired, an' I want to go to bed;
But first I want to talk to You 'bout some things I said
Today to Bobby Jones who lives across the line.
He don't have many playthings; so he comes and plays
   with mine.

[32]

This morning he come over 'fore I was even dressed
And asked my Ma if he could play with my bran' new
    express.
While I was eating breakfast he raced it 'round so hard
The back wheel lost its tire right there in our front yard.

Then I got out my sponge ball; he lost it in the weeds;
My story book went in the brook; he broke my sister's
    beads.
An' then, dear Lord, I got real mad an' said some things I
    know
That made my Ma ashamed of me; she said they wasn't so.

She made me 'pologize to Bob; o' course that made me
    weep.
Dear God, it seems I'm awful bad, an' I can't go to sleep
Unless You will forgive me, Lord, an' teach me how to play;
An' bless my playmate Bobby Jones. Please teach me how
    to pray.

JAMES W. STANISTREET

❖ ❖ ❖

THE FLY IN CHURCH

My Aunties on each side of me are kneeling in a line;
I wonder if their hassocks are as full of pins as mine?
I think they must have asked the hens to teach them how to
    perch;
I'd like to rub knees, but that's called fidgeting in Church.

I found a fly in Church today — a fly who'd hurt his wing;
It happened just as everyone was standing up to sing
"There's a Friend for little children up above the bright
    blue sky" —
I might have been so good if they had let me keep that fly.

I thought of such a lovely game — I didn't fidget then —
The fly must walk across my book before I counted ten;
But just as he was nearly there the Man said, "Let us
   pray,"
And Aunties shook their heads at me and brushed my fly
   away.

The pew is very dark and high, and I am very small,
And Aunties say it's wrong in Church to look about at all.
I think the window's open where the glass is painted red,
For I can feel a scrap of sky that's shining on my head.

Oh Friend for little children, You were once as small as me,
You know how very, very dull a child in Church can be,
And if You're hiding just above that tiny patch of sky,
Be sorry for a little boy — and send another fly!

JOCELYN C. LEA

❖ ❖ ❖

THE FOOLISH LITTLE SHADOW

I was a little shadow,
I sat upon a wall,
I made a little jump for glee,
And then I had a fall.

I fell into a butter-cup
Upon the meadow brown,
The goblins came and helped me up
And told of my renown.

Oh, foolish little shadow,
To be so bold and gay;
Pride always has to have a fall —
There is no other way.

EMILY K. SOLLIDAY

FOR FRIENDS OF PETER PAN

I know that there are fairies
For every time I see
A mirror shining in the sun
Peter Pan just smiles at me.

And when the moon is shining down
And everything is bright
Some folks see just moonlight
But I know it's Peter's light.

LAURA WRIGHT

❖ ❖ ❖

GETTING ACQUAINTED

I got acquainted very quick
With Teddy Brown, when he
Moved in the house across the street —
The nearest one, you see.

I climbed and sat upon a post
To look, and so did he;
I stared and stared across at him,
And he stared back at me.

I s'posed he wanted me to speak;
I thought I'd try and see.
I said " Hello! " to Teddy Brown;
He said " Hello! " to me.

SYDNEY DAYRE

THE HAPPINESS FAIRY

Have you seen the little fairy,
That lives in the mossy dell?
She dances in the moonlight;
Have you seen her, pray now, tell.

She comes to sing to the blossoms,
That grow on the old cherry tree;
She solves for the birds their problems,
Of how to be glad, and free.

I know that you will see her,
If you keep your eye fixed right;
She seems to wink at the daisies,
When you are asleep at night.

I know that you will hear her,
If you're always kind and true;
She's singing for the bob-o-link,
She'll sing as well for you.

I've heard the little fairy,
And oh! her song is so sweet!
You might hear her when the raindrops
Come dancing down at your feet.

I hope that you will see her,
And hear her too, I guess, —
She is the dearest fairy,
She makes our happiness.

EMILY K. SOLLIDAY

THE HELPFUL FAIRY

Today when I gathered the pansies — I saw such a wonderful thing;
A dear little mite of a fairy was mending a butterfly's wing!
She sewed with a thorn and a cobweb — and did it so gently,
the dear!
(Yet some folks say the fairies aren't useful. You just can't
believe all you hear!)

SALLY JOHNSON

❖ ❖ ❖

" IFS "

IF I had wings I would fly afar;
IF I were a fairy I would light a star;
IF I had a ship I would sail away,
And in some foreign country stay;
But, IF is a word both small and great,
And leaves us all in a very bad state.

LOUISE BARRETT (9 years)

❖ ❖ ❖

I WISH

I wish I was a pickaninny,
Black as coal dust, so
That I could skip my bath sometimes,
And Ma would never know.

KATHRYN REINHARD

Good-by, little birdie!
  Fly to the sky,
Singing and singing
  A merry good-by.

Tell all the birdies
  Flying above,
Jane, in the garden,
  Sends them her love.

Tell how I found you,
  Hurt in a tree;
Then, when they're wounded,
  They'll come right to me.

I'd like to go with you,
  If I could fly;
It must be so beautiful
  Up in the sky!

Why, little birdie —
  Why don't you go?
You sit on my finger,
  And shake your head, " No! "

He's off! Oh, how quickly
  And gladly he rose!
I know he will love me
  Wherever he goes.

I know — for he really
  Seemed trying to say:
" My dear little Janie,
  I can't go away."

But just then some birdies
  Came flying along,
And sang, as they neared us,
  A chirruping song:

And he felt just as I do
  When girls come and shout
Right under the window,
  " Come, Janie — come out! "

It's wrong to be sorry;
  I ought to be glad;
But he's the best birdie
  That ever I had.

MARY MAPES DODGE

❖ ❖ ❖

LORD, TEACH A LITTLE CHILD

Lord, teach a little child to pray,
  And, oh, accept my prayer.
Thou hearest all the words I say,
  For Thou art everywhere.

A little sparrow cannot fall
  Unnoticed, Lord, by Thee;
And though I am so young and small,
  Thou carest still for me.

Teach me to do what is right,
  And when I sin, forgive;
And make it still my chief delight
  To love Thee while I live.

THE 'LUSIVE FAIRY

One night I saw a fairy (I did)
  Down by the garden wall,
But when I went to catch her
  She wasn't there at all.

I've looked in every flower
  And behind each blade of grass,
But all that I have found
  Are the fireflies sailing past.

And so each night when the moon is high
  And the stars are shining brightly,
I go and look by the garden wall
  For I've yet to find that fairy. (Well, I will.)

BETTY SOLLIDAY

❖ ❖ ❖

THE ANGEL

A thing I cannot see
  Is a spirit.
It flies about me like a bee.
  'Tis a spirit.

Like a root you cannot see
  Is a spirit.
Like the sweetness in my tea
  Is a spirit.

CARL HORN (11 years)

ANOTHER

Hello, hello, to Ed and Dave!
  Hello, to Edith too!
You're a mighty fine batch
  Of mighty fine kids —
But just hear Bobby coo-oo!

ANN BUDDY

❖ ❖ ❖

MY MOTHER'S STORIES

I love to romp with doggie,
And play with pussy-cat;
But to hear my mother's stories —
Gee — nothin' can beat that!
I always love to hear them
But they seem the best at night,
When mother takes me on her lap
And holds me close and tight;
She tells me all about the stars,
And — oh, such lovely things,
Why skies are blue — how flowers grow,
'Bout magic fairy rings.
She tells me all about the rain,
And where the rivers run;
But when she tells me the " Three Bears "
Oh, that's the mostest fun!
Big Bear goes — " GRRR " — and my, oh my!
I hug quite close to ma!
But when the Little Bear goes — " grrr "
I'm brave and laugh ha-ha!
I love to romp with puppy-dog,
And play with pussy-cat,
But to hear my mother's stories —
Gee — nothin' can beat that!

RUTH HECKMAN

MY NURSERY WALLS

If I wake up
Before anyone calls,
I count all the things
On my nursery walls.

First there come,
Each waving his trunk,
Three gray elephants,
Plunk! Plunk!
And after them,
Making a fuss,
A puffing
Hippopotamus!
A superior camel
Kneels in the sand,
And two giraffes
Close by him stand
Stretching
Their long, long necks
With ease
To browse the leaves
From the tops of trees!
A kangaroo
And a red flamingo
Gravely stare
At a prowling dingo:
While
Three downy ducklings,
All in a row,
Over a path
To the water go;
And then, again,
Each waving his trunk,
Come my nice elephants,
Plunk! Plunk!

I travel around,
And around the walls
If I wake up
Before anyone calls!

AILEEN BEAUFORT

❖ ❖ ❖

MY TREASURE

Pirates for their treasure
Have a chest of yellow gold
And as they plunder ships at sea
They look so brave and bold
But I'm just a little boy
And cannot go to sea
But I have a treasure too
Finer than gold can be
My treasure is a person
And a loving one you know
And I'll guard my priceless wealth
Against the evils of the foe
For if I lose this treasure
I cannot get another
I suppose you've guessed by this time
My treasure is my mother.

MARVIN COOKE

❖ ❖ ❖

MY VERY DEAR

First thing I see each morning
When the Sandman leaves my eyes
Is the frizzy white toy poodle
That lies cuddled to my side.

He's mighty good for company
All through the spooky night
But no one would be scared of him
'Cause toy dogs they don't bite.

MARY FAITH

❖ ❖ ❖

MR. FINNEY'S TURNIP

Mr. Finney had a turnip
 And it grew and it grew;
And it grew behind the barn
 And that turnip did no harm.

There it grew and it grew
 Till it could grow no longer;
Then his daughter Lizzie picked it
 And put it in the cellar.

There it lay and it lay
 Till it began to rot;
And his daughter Susie took it
 And put it in the pot.

And they boiled it and boiled it
 As long as they were able,
And then his daughters took it
 And put it on the table.

Mr. Finney and his wife
 They sat down to sup:
And they ate and they ate
 And they ate that turnip up.

HENRY W. LONGFELLOW

NEARLY

Into the room
I crept so soft —
I scarcely breathed,
And I never coughed —
So soft, they could hardly
Know I was there,
Into the room
With oh, such care
I crept — that I nearly
Broke their Law,
They were just in time,
But I nearly saw!

Out in the dark
I stood so still —
Like a bit of the door
Or the window sill —
So still, they could hardly
Think of me,
Out in the dark
So noiselessly
I stood — that I nearly
Got the Word,
They were just in time,
But I nearly heard!

Down in the wood
I tried so hard —
Hoping to get them
Off their guard,
So hard they could scarcely
Get away,
Down in the wood
So hard the day

I tried — that I nearly
Got right through,
They were just in time,
But I nearly knew!

ELEANOR FARJEON

❖ ❖ ❖

THE NIGHT

Why is it that I have to sleep
And cannot lie awake
To listen to the many sounds
That every night can make?

Why is it I can only see
The moon start on her path
And then be told right after that
To rise and take a bath?

When Mummy comes to hear my prayers
And kiss me fond good-night
To tuck me nicely into bed
And turn out all the light

It hardly takes a minute for
Some queer sound to be heard
That rushes through the still cool dark
Or seems all hushed and blurred.

But the night will never tell me,
She sends me right to sleep
And keeps my eyelids closed all night
Without a chance to peep.

I hope some day, when I grow up,
That I can hear and see
The sights and sounds that the dear night
Has always hid from me.

POLLY KING

❖ ❖ ❖

OH DEAR

I often wish that I had wings
Just like the birds that fly and sing.
They sing and sing and never fail
And never have to practice scales.

KATY LOU TUCK

❖ ❖ ❖

PARTNERSHIP

You needn't be looking around at me so,
She's my kitten as much as your kitten you know,
And I'll take her wherever I wish her to go!

You know very well that, the day she was found,
If I hadn't cried, she'd surely been drowned;
And you ought to be thankful she's here safe and sound!

She's only crying 'cause she's a goose.
I'm not squeezing her; look now, my arms are quite loose,
And she may as well hush, for it's not any use.

And you may as well get right down and go 'way;
You're not in this thing we're going to play;
And remember it isn't your half of the day.

You're forgetting the bargain we made, and so soon!
In the morning she's mine, and yours all afternoon.
And you couldn't teach her to eat with a spoon.

So don't let me hear one single mew!
Do you know what will happen right off if you do?
She'll be my kitten mornings and afternoons too!

❖ ❖ ❖

THE REASON

The other day I saw a worm,
A nice fat woolly one.
It oozed and turned and squeezed and squirmed,
To watch it was such fun.
His back was brown and kind of spreckled,
His head was sort of red.
I think he must have been all freckled
'Cause the sun's the covers on his bed.

ISABEL RENNIE

❖ ❖ ❖

THE RAIN

Rain, rain,
    On the window pane —
Splitter, splatter
    What a noise!
Now the children can't play
With their outdoor toys.

Rain, rain,
    Why do you fall?
        Aren't you tired
    Without resting at all?

Now I count the falling fairies
    One, two, three, four —
Oh, there are hundreds and thousands
    And more.

Rain, rain,
    On the window pane —
Splitter, splatter
    What a noise!
Now the children can't play
With their outdoor toys.

CLARK DILL MOORE (7 years)

❖ ❖ ❖

RAIN ON A TIN ROOF

When it began to rain
Yesterday,
I thought it was the fairies
Playing tinners,
Tinning the roof
With their little hammers.

HERMAN LIVEZEY

❖ ❖ ❖

THE RAINBOW IN THE STREET

I saw a piece of rainbow
    That the rainbow fairies dropped.
It was lying in the street
    After all the rain had stopped.

My brother said that it was oil
    That wouldn't mix with H_2O
But I'm sure that rainbow fairies
    Dropped a piece of the rainbow.

LUCILE MURRAY

SEVEN TIMES ONE

There's no dew left on the daisies and clover,
    There's no rain left in heaven.
I've said my " seven times " over and over,
    Seven times one are seven.

I am old, so old I can write a letter,
    My birthday lessons are done.
The lambs play always, they know no better,
    They are only one times one.

O moon!   In the night I have seen you sailing
    And shining so round and low;
You were bright, oh bright! but your light is failing,
    You are nothing now but a bow.

You moon, have you done something wrong in heaven
    That God has hidden your face?
I hope if you have you will soon be forgiven
    And shine again in your place.

O velvet bee, you're a dusty fellow,
    You've powdered your legs with gold.
O brave marshmary buds rich and yellow,
    Give me your money to hold.

O columbine, open your folded wrapper
    Where two twin turtledoves dwell;
O cuckoo, toll me the purple clapper
    That hangs in your green bell.

And show me your nest with the young ones in it
    I will not steal it away.
I am old, you may trust me linnet,
    I am seven times one today.

JEAN INGELOW

[50]

SOME MAN

Bobby is a baby
Who's going to be a man.
He's growing bigger every day
As promptly as he can.

He eats his milk and spinach,
His carrots and his grool —
In 5 more years he means to be
The biggest boy in school.

He has a great big chest for breath
And great big hands to whack —
In 10 more years he means to be
A great big quarterback.

He has a great big gorgeous smile
And not a single frown,
He has a great big head to think,
    (All baldish on the crown) —
In 15 years he means to be
The nicest man in town.

My Bobby is a baby
Who aims to be Some Man!
He's growing bigger every day
As promptly as he can.

ANN BUDDY

❖ ❖ ❖

THE SUFFRAGETTE

When I grow up I 'spect to be
A Drug Store Man, because you see
I'll have lots of candy and licorice sweet
And ice cream sodas and fudge to eat.

I'll have stamps in a drawer and postcards gay
And packs of money that people pay.
I'll give little boys powders bad as I can.
I'm a girl — but I'll grow
    To a Drug Store Man.

GRACE DRAYTON

❖   ❖   ❖

SUNRISE

Every day old Mr. Sun
Climbs on his way up
Into the bright blue sky.
When the moon sees him
She waves good-bye;
And all the baby stars
Nod their drowsy heads
And then go to sleep
In their bright blue beds.

CLARK DILL MOORE (7 years)

❖   ❖   ❖

THERE WAS A LITTLE GIRL

There was a little girl,
And she had a little curl
    Right in the middle of her forehead.
When she was good
She was very, very good,
    And when she was bad she was horrid!

One day she went upstairs,
When her parents, unawares,

[52]

In the kitchen were occupied with meals.
And she stood upon her head
In her little trundle-bed,
   And then began hooraying with her heels.

Her mother heard the noise,
And she thought it was the boys
   A-playing at a combat in the attic;
But when she climbed the stair
And found Jemima there,
   She took and she did spank her most emphatic!
                                    HENRY W. LONGFELLOW

❖ ❖ ❖

A TROUBLESOME CHILD

My Maud Louise is a Paris doll
   With the cunningest turned up nose,
And four white teeth, and a parasol
   And lace all over her clothes.

And goodness, isn't she the worst!
   She's never a moment still —
She sucked my red balloon till it burst,
   Of course she was deathly ill.

She's always running away to hide
   On purpose to make me search;
She jumps on wagons to steal a ride
   And giggles aloud in Church!

She broke the blade of my pocket knife,
   I haven't a dish uncracked.
Why every day of her naughty life
   She has to be simply whacked.

I'm just discouraged. Won't some of you
    Whose dollies are good and mild
Please write to me telling me what to do
    To manage this dreadful child?

❖ ❖ ❖

TROUBLE IN THE KITCHEN

When Mary to the kitchen went
    After school one night
She found that all the kitchen things
    Were in a dreadful plight.

She found the bread just rising
    The onions in a stew
The cabbage in a pickle
    The jelly quivering too.

The kitchen window had a pane
    The gas had just flared out
The vinegar looked very sour
    No one knew what about.

The kitchen clock was so ashamed
    To see its friends' disgrace
It stopped quite still and sadly held
    Its hands before its face.

❖ ❖ ❖

TO TOMMY

Anne Ellen is our baby's name
'Twas on last Saturday she came
But I don't think she's very pretty
I much prefer my little kitty.

It can run, an' play, an' climb
That baby sleeps most all the time
An' when it doesn't, just cries and cries
An' never seems to open its eyes.
I asked the Doctor to bring one older
Then I went upstairs an' told 'er
If she didn't get up an' come out an' play
I wasn't gonna let her stay.

LAURA HEEBNER BESTER

❖ ❖ ❖

WHAT THE ACORN SAID

" My, I think I heard a raindrop,"
Said an acorn half awake.
" Time that I was up and doing
For I have an oak to make."

RUTH DAINS (11 years)

❖ ❖ ❖

WHEN I WAS SMALL

When I was very little
I used to think, my dear,
That people meant kind railroad men
When they said, " Civil engineer."

LAURA WRIGHT

WHERE THE SPANKWEED GROWS

There's a corner in our garden, but our nurse won't tell me
    where
That little boys must never see, but always must beware
And in that corner all the year in rows and rows and rows,
A drefful little flower called the
        Spankweed grows!

My nurse says that if a boy who doesn't wash his face,
Or pulls his little sister's hair should ever find that place,
That Spankweed just would jump at him and dust his little
    clothes,
Oh!   It's never safe for fellers where the
        Spankweed grows!

Some day I'll get the sickle from our hired man and then
I'll go and find the Spankweed place, it's somewhere in the
    glen,
And when I get a swingin' it and puttin' in *my* blows,
I bet there'll be excitement where the
        Spankweed grows.

☼　☼　☼　☼　☼　☼　☼　☼　☼　☼

POEMS FOR
INTERMEDIATE GRADES

ON THE WAY HOME

S'posin' you do stub your toe, Emmy Lou,
'Taint nothin' if you do,
'Taint no use to yell
Like you thought it would come in two.
Goodness me, if I was you
I'd laugh an' say
Pooh, 'taint nothin'!

S'posin' you do see a cow what hollers moo,
'Taint nothin' if you do.
'Taint no use to run like you
Was most scared to death.
Say shoo! that's the way I always do.
Stand right still and holler shoo!
'Taint nothin'!

S'posin' you do hear a lion, Emmy Lou,
'Taint nothin' real for true —
It's just a shadder —
Gee, I sure heard somethin' then, Emmy Lou,
D-d-d-didn't you?
L-l-let's try an' see which one can beat.
Come on!   Let's run!
T-t-taint nothin'!

❖ ❖ ❖

A TEN–YEAR–OLD'S VACATION

I thought it would be fun to go
Away from home, and it would be,
But there are two I'm missing so.
I wish they could be here with me.

When we are home we disagree.
It's funny now I am away
How very much I long to see
My brother Harry and Marie,
And run with them and laugh and play.

I s'pose when I go home again
I'll tell them that I had such fun,
And never mention how in vain
I longed for them from sun to sun
To play " Red Light " and " Run Sheep Run "
And all the games we know so well.
But I expect I'll kiss each one,
And then we'll scrap — and I'll tell none
Of those sweet things I want to tell!

ANNE CAMPBELL

❖ ❖ ❖

THE LOST DOLL

I once had a sweet little doll, dears,
    The prettiest doll in the world;
Her cheeks were so red and so white, dears,
    And her hair was so charmingly curled.

But I lost my poor little doll, dears,
    As I played on the heath one day;
And I cried for more than a week, dears,
    But I never could find where she lay.

I found my poor little doll, dears
    As I played on the heath one day;
Folks say she is terribly changed, dears,
    For her paint is all washed away;

And her arms trodden off by the cows, dears,
    And her hair not the least bit curled;
Yet for old sake's sake, she is still, dears,
    The prettiest doll in the world.

CHARLES KINGSLEY

❖ ❖ ❖

MRS. GRAMMAR'S BALL

Mrs. Good Grammar gave a fine ball,
To the nine different parts of our speech;
    To the big and the small,
    To the short and the tall,
There were dainties, favors and bonbons for each.

And first little Articles came,
In a hurry to make themselves known —
    Fat A, An and The;
    But none of the three
Could stand for a minute alone.

The Adjectives came to announce
That their dear friends the Nouns were at hand,
    Rough, Rougher, Roughest,
    Tough, Tougher, Toughest,
Fat, Merry, Good-natured and Grand.

The Nouns were indeed on their way —
Tens of thousands and more, I should think,
    For each name that we utter —
    Shop, Shoulder, or Shutter —
Is a noun, Lady, Lyon and Link.

The Pronouns were following fast
To push the Nouns out of their places —
    I, Thou, You and Me,
    We, They, He and She,
With their merry, good-humored old faces.

Some cried, " Make way for the Verbs! "
A great crowd is coming in view —
　　To Bite and To Smite,
　　And To Light and To Fight,
To Be and To Have and To Do.

The Adverbs attend on the Verbs,
Behind them as footmen they run;
　　As thus, To Fight Badly,
　　They Run Away Gladly,
Shows how fighting and running were done.

Prepositions came — In, By and Near,
With Conjunctions, a poor little band,
　　As Either you Or me,
　　But Neither they Nor he —
They held their great friends by the hand.

Then in with a " Hip, hip, hurrah! "
Rushed Interjections uproarious —
　　" Oh, dear! Well a day! "
　　When they saw the display,
" Ha! ha! " they all shouted out, " Glorious! "

❖　❖　❖

GRATITUDE

I see so many lovely things
　　I can't express in words —
The lake, the hills, the sky, the sun,
　　The flowers, trees, and birds.

I see a glorious sunset,
　　I wander through a wood;
I think so many lovely thoughts,
　　I'd tell them if I could.

It's useless; all that I can do
  Is try to live my love,
To show my gratitude by care
  Of God's gifts from above.

POLLY HUNTER

❖ ❖ ❖

THE CHILD'S DREAM

Last night before I fell asleep,
I thought I heard God go
Down the long corridor,
Slow — slow — slow.

He came near — and — nearer —
But the next that I knew
The sun was streaming in my room
And the sky was April-blue.

But later, picking cowslips
Down by the stream,
I suddenly remembered
That I had had a dream.

But how was I to tell it
In any kind of words
When the nearest thing to Raphael
That we have are wings and birds?

And how to tell the colors
When the nearest things we know
To the blue and white of Mary's dress
Are April skies and snow?

For something more golden
Than suns had poured about.
I had heard a great singing
Within me and without.

Then the brook answered me
And, tumbling into words,
It said: " Immanuel singing
Was what you heard."

Then the birds fell a-twittering
Though it was broad day,
And not a passing beetle
Hurried from my way.

And a voice like a white birch,
Like joy and like awe,
Said in silver: " It was He
That you heard and saw! "

Then there came a chorus
From the sky-rim
And from the meadow mushrooms:
" She has seen Him! "

ISABEL FISKE CONANT

❖   ❖   ❖

THE LITTLE BLACK BOY

My mother bore me in the southern wild,
    And I am black, but O, my soul is white!
White as an angel is the English child,
    But I am black, as if bereaved of light.

My mother taught me underneath a tree,
    And sitting down before the heat of day,
She took me on her lap and kissed me,
    And pointing to the East, began to say:

" Look at the rising sun; there God does live,
    And gives His light, and gives His heat away,
And flowers and trees and beasts and men receive
    Comfort in morning, joy in the noonday.

" And we are put on earth a little space,
    That we may learn to bear the beams of love;
And these black bodies and this sunburnt face
    Are but a cloud, and like a shady grave.

" For when our souls have learn'd the heat to bear,
    The cloud will vanish, we shall hear His voice,
Saying, " Come out from the grave, my love and care
    And round my golden tent like lambs rejoice."

Thus did my mother say, and kissed me,
    And thus I say to little English boy.
When I from black and he from white cloud free,
    And round the tent of God like lambs we joy,

I'll shade him from the heat till he can bear
    To lean in joy upon our Father's knee;
And then I'll stand and stroke his silver hair,
    And be like him, and he will then love me.

WILLIAM BLAKE

❖   ❖   ❖

A CHILD'S THOUGHT OF GOD

They say that God lives very high!
    But if you look above the pines
You cannot see our God. And why?

And if you dig down in the mines
   You never see him in the gold,
Though from Him all that's glory shines.

God is so good He wears a fold
   Of heaven and earth across His face —
Like secrets kept, for love, untold.

But still I feel that His embrace
   Slides down by thrills, through all things made,
Through sight and sound of every place;

As if my tender mother laid
   On my shut lids, her kisses' pressure,
Half-waking me at night; and said
    "Who kissed you through the dark, dear guesser?"
                ELIZABETH BARRETT BROWNING

❖ ❖ ❖

A SONG FROM THE SUDS

Queen of my tub, I merrily sing
While the white foam rises high,
And sturdily wash and rinse and wring,
And fasten the clothes to dry;
And then out in the fresh air they swing
Under the sunny sky.

I wish we could wash from our hearts and our souls
The stains of the week away,
And let pure water and air by their magic make
Ourselves as pure as they;
Then on the earth there would be, indeed,
A glorious washing day!

Along the path of a useful life
Will heart's ease ever bloom;
The busy mind has no time to think
Of sorrow, or care, or gloom;
And anxious thoughts may be swept away
As we busily wield a broom.

I am glad a task to me is given
To labor at day by day;
For it brings me health and strength and hope,
And I cheerfully learn to say:
"Head, you may think; heart, you may feel;
But, hand, you shall work always!"

LOUISA M. ALCOTT (at fifteen)

❖   ❖   ❖

THE LADY OF THE LAMBS

She walks — the lady of my delight —
    A shepherdess of sheep.
Her flocks are thoughts. She keeps them white;
    She guards them from the steep;
She feeds them on the fragrant height,
    And folds them in for sleep.

She roams maternal hills and bright,
    Dark valleys safe and deep.
Into that tender breast at night
    The chastest stars may peep.
She walks — the lady of my delight —
    A shepherdess of sheep.

[67]

She holds her little thoughts in sight,
    Though gay they run and leap.
She is so circumspect and right
    She has her soul to keep.
She walks — the lady of my delight —
    A shepherdess of sheep.

ALICE MEYNELL

❖   ❖   ❖

THE LITTLE SHEPHERD'S SONG

(thirteenth century)

The leaves, the little birds and I,
The fleece clouds and the sweet, sweet sky,
The pages singing as they ride
Down there, down there where the river is wide.
Heigh-ho, what a day!   What a lovely day!
Even too lovely to hop and play
With my sheep
Or sleep
In the sun!

And so I lie in the deep grass
And watch the pages as they pass.
And sing to them as they to me
Till they turn the bend by the poplar tree.
And then — oh, then I sing right on
To the leaves and the lambs and myself alone!
    For I think there must be
        Inside of me
            A bird!

WILLIAM A. PERCY

THE SOUTH WIND

(from Hiawatha)

Shawondasee, fat and lazy,
Had his dwelling far to southward,
In the drowsy, dreamy sunshine,
In the never-ending summer.
He it was who sent the wood-birds,
Sent the robin, the Opechee,
Sent the bluebird, the Owaissa,
Sent the Shawshaw, sent the swallow,
Sent the wild goose, Wawa, northward
Sent the melons and tobacco,
And the grapes in purple clusters.

From his pipe the smoke ascending
Filled the sky with haze and vapor,
Filled the air with dreamy softness,
Gave a twinkle to the water,
Touched the rugged hills with smoothness,
Brought the tender Indian Summer
To the melancholy North-land,
In the dreary Moon of Snow-Shoes.

Listless, careless Shawondasee!
In his life he had one shadow,
In his heart one sorrow had he.
Once as he was gazing northward,
Far away upon the prairie;
Brightest green were all her garments,
And her hair was like the sunshine.

Day by day he gazed upon her,
Day by day he sighed with passion,
Day by day his heart within him
Grew more hot with love and longing
For the maid with yellow tresses.

But he was too fat and lazy
To bestir himself and woo her:
Yes, too indolent and easy
To pursue her and persuade her,
Only sat and sighed with passion
For the maiden of the prairie.

Till one morning, looking northward,
He beheld her yellow tresses
Changed and covered o'er with whiteness,
Covered as with whitest snow-flakes.
" Ah! my brother from the North-land,
From the kingdom of Wabasso,
From the land of the White Rabbit!
You have stolen the maiden from me,
You have laid your hand upon her,
You have wooed and won my maiden,
With your stories of the North-land! "

Thus the wretched Shawondasee
Breathed into the air his sorrow;
And the South-wind o'er the prairie
Wandered warm with sighs of passion,
With the sighs of Shawondasee,
Till the air seemed full of snow-flakes,
Full of thistle-down the prairie,
And the maid with hair like sunshine
Vanished from his sight forever;
Nevermore did Shawondasee
See the maid with yellow tresses!

Poor deluded Shawondasee!
'Twas no woman that you gazed at,
'Twas no maiden that you sighed for,
'Twas the prairie dandelion

That through all the dreamy summer
You had gazed at with such longing,
You had sighed for with such passion,
And had puffed away forever,
Blown into the air with sighing.
Ah! deluded Shawondasee!

HENRY W. LONGFELLOW

❖ ❖ ❖

A GAY GREEN FAIRY

A gay green fairy
  Wove a jig
Over a pebble
  Under a twig.

Slid down a grass blade,
  Stamped at a bug;
Into a worm's den
  Dark and snug,

Puffed with a dew-ball
  Up a slope;
Into an ant hole
  To bits it broke.

Rolled for joy
  Under a nettle;
Jumped with fright
  Away from a beetle.

Straddled a bee's back
  Fuzzy with pollen,
Pulled his ear
  Loudly calling —

"Why do I weave
   A jig today?
I weave a jig
   Because I am gay!"

DORCAS LITTLEFIELD

❖ ❖ ❖

A LAUGHING CHORUS

Oh, such a commotion under the ground
   When March called, "Ho there! Ho!"
Such spreading of rootlets far and wide,
   Such whisperings to and fro.
And "Are you ready?" the Snowdrop asked;
   "'Tis time to start you know."
"Almost, my dear," the Scilla replied;
   "I'll follow as soon as you go."
Then, "Ha! ha!" a chorus came
   Of laughter soft and low
From the millions of flowers under the ground —
   Yes — millions — beginning to grow.

"I'll promise my blossoms," the Crocus said,
   "When I hear the bluebirds sing."
And straight thereafter Narcissus cried,
   "My silver and gold I'll bring."
"And ere they are dulled," another spoke,
   "The Hyacinth bells shall ring."
And the Violet only murmured, "I'm here;"
   And sweet grew the air of Spring.
Then "Ha! ha! ha!" a chorus came
   Of laughter soft and low
From the millions of flowers under the ground —
   Yes — millions — beginning to grow.

Oh, the pretty brave things! through the coldest days,
   Imprisoned in walls of brown,
They never lost heart, though the blast shrieked loud,
   And the sleet and hail came down,
But patiently each wrought her beautiful dress,
   Or fashioned her beautiful crown;
And now they are coming to brighten the world,
   Still shadowed by winter's frown;
And well they may cheerily laugh " Ha! ha! "
   In a chorus soft and low,
The millions of flowers hid under the ground —
   Yes — millions — beginning to grow.

❖ ❖ ❖

THE AWAKENING

Do you like daisies and lambs with long tails?
   Meadows and April and gold buttercups?
Send for the South Wind — his knock never fails —
   Tell him to waken Persephone up,
Tell him to say to her dimples and curls,
That slug-a-bed habits don't suit little girls.

Nonsense, he can't have forgotten the road,
   Hasn't he called her, oh often before?
Well then, old Pluto's black marble abode,
   Well then, the keyhole (best choose the back door)
Now let him tip-toe a corridor's gloom,
Turn to the left and he's facing her room.

Here, if again through a keyhole he'll sweep,
   Little Persephone sweetly he'll scan,
Lying like snow and wild roses, asleep,
   Now he must whisper, as only he can,
" Daisies," and, presently (this never fails
If " Daisies " don't waken her), " Lambs with long tails."

Then let him hasten, I'd not have him there
    When neat little knuckles are rubbing blue eyes
And she sits up in bed to push back her bright hair
    And blink at the clock in a pretty surprise;
Yes, it won't take him two of her cuckoo clock's ticks
To be off through both keyholes and back across Styx.

But we'll know that she's waking, for over the way
    The thrush on the apple tree says so at once;
And didn't the bells of the snow-drops today
    Fair tingle and jingle, and does not each dunce
That hears that tink-tinkle, that thin one, two, three,
Know that little Persephone rings for her tea?

PATRICK R. CHALMERS

❖   ❖   ❖

THE DAISY ELF

" He loves me
Un peu, beaucoup,
Passionement, point-du-tout."
The little maiden slowly said
Pulling from the daisy's head
The long white petals. And just then,
As she reached the eleventh one,
From the yellow center part
From the daisy's very heart
Stepped a tiny elf.
" Why, I'm counting those myself! "
Said the roguish little fellow
Perched upon the breast of yellow.

" Passionately,
You have gone just to there
Finish quickly, but take care
Make it come out well. 'Tis so

That I'm in love myself, you know
And I tell the truth this once —
But go on you little dunce! "
Then the wondering little maid
Pulled the others, half afraid
'Till it came out " Point-du-tout,"
But what could the maiden do?

" Not at all?
That's not true! " the midget said
And angrily he shook his head,
Stamped his tiny foot and from
The edge of gold, another one
Another petal pure and white
Came from somewhere into sight.
The little man then laughed in glee.
" Un peu, that makes it now," said he.
" But from a little there will come
More love for us and everyone.
So my fairy I shall wed
And light steps to music tread!

" Adieu, adieu."
Then right down the stem he slid
Disappearing as he did,
And the astonished little maid
Whom his highness had waylaid
Gathered up the petals there,
Counted all of them again,
Found indeed the magic one
Which " un peu " had just begun
And she smiled because she knew
For her 'twould ne'er be " point-du-tout."

DORA ADÉLE SHOEMAKER

THE FLOWERS' BALL

There is an olden story;
'Tis a legend so I'm told,
How the flowers gave a banquet,
In the ivied days of old;
How the posies gave a party once
That wound up with a ball,
How they held it in the valley,
Down in Flowery Kingdom Hall.

The flowers of every clime were there,
Of high and low degree,
All with their petals polished,
In sweet aromatic glee;
They met down in this woodland,
In the soft and ambient air,
Each in its lolling loveliness,
Exhaled a perfume rare.

The orchestra of Blue Bells
Sat upon a mossy knoll
And pealed forth gentle music
That quite captured every soul.
The Holly hocked a pistol
Just to buy a suit of clothes
And danced with all the flowers
But the modest blushing Rose.

The Morning Glory shining
Seemed reflecting all the glow
Of dawn, and took a partner;
It was young Miss Mistletoe.
Miss Maggie Nolia from the South
Danced with Forget-Me-Not;
Sweet William took Miss Pink in tow
And danced a slow gavotte.

Thus everything went swimmingly
'Mongst perfumed belles and beaux;
And every flower reveled save
The modest, blushing Rose.
Miss Fuchsia sat around and told
For floral emulation,
That she actually refused
To dance with A. Carnation.

The Coxcomb, quite a dandy there,
Began to pine and mope,
Until he had been introduced
To young Miss Heliotrope.
Sir Cactus took Miss Lily,
And he swung her so about
She asked Sweet Pea to Cauliflower
And put the Cactus out.

Miss Pansy took her Poppy,
And she waltzed him down the line
Till they ran against old Sunflower
With Miss Honeysuckle Vine.
The others at the party that
Went whirling through the mazy
Were the Messrs. Rhodo Dendron,
Daffodil and Little Daisy.

Miss Petunia, Miss Verbena, Violet,
And sweet Miss Dahlia,
Came fashionably late, arrayed
In very rich regalia.
Miss Begonia, sweet Miss Buttercup,
Miss Lilac, and Miss Clover,
Young Dandelion came in late
When all the feast was over.

The only flower that sent regrets
And really couldn't come,
Who lived in the four hundred, was
The vain Chrysanthemum.
One flower at the table
Grew quite ill, we must regret,
And every posy wondered too,
Just what Miss Mignon-ette.

Young Tulip chose Miss Orchid
From the first and did not part
With her until Miss Marigold
Fell with a Bleeding Heart.
But ah! Miss Rose sat pensively
Till every young lad passed her.
Then just to fill the last quadrille
The little China Aster.

❖   ❖   ❖

A PARTY

The oak tree gave a party for
The leaves, one autumn day.
They changed their old green summer clothes
To gold and crimson gay.

Their friends, the birds, were asked to come,
But they had no new dress,
" We thank you, we are going South
By early crane express."

" What will we do for music now? "
The poor tree hung its head.
The kind wind felt sorry too —
" I'll blow for you," he said.

He whistled the most merry tunes
And blew and blew and blew,
Till all the leaves thought they were birds,
And far away they flew.

LOUISA J. BROOKER

❖   ❖   ❖

MAGNOLIA TREE

I saw you last winter
With your white bark boots on
Standing in the snow,
Drinking in the glow
Of the moon,
And counting the points
On the stars.
You were fingering something
You had caught in the wind,
And were packing it into little buds.
And now you bloom —
Your blossoms are full of snow,
Stamens of stars,
And the glow
Of the moon.

HERMAN LIVEZEY

❖   ❖   ❖

PRIDE

The maple trees one autumn day
Whispered in such a funny way
I stopped to listen to them say;

" Oh, dear, oh dear, our hair so green
Has lost its color and its sheen
And we are old and worn and mean."

[79]

And then those silly trees, my dear,
Dyed their hair one morning clear
And dried it in the sun for cheer.

Soon when a breeze went dancing by
They shook their curls with pride, oh fie —
And tossed bright heads with scorn on high.

That frisky breeze called brothers three,
They blew and blew, 'till now, ah me —
Those haughty trees are bald, you see.

ANNE BELL

❖ ❖ ❖

PEACH-BLOOMS

Peach-blossoms always seem to me
Like fairy dreams upon a tree.

They are so lovely, primly pink
They make me think — and think — and think!

I think of them as children's thought
Within a bunch of branches caught;

Or maybe they are fairies' wings
Entangled in God's scheme of things.

I often wonder if they grow
Because we children love them so,

Or, if they merely happened there
To make us children sit and stare!

MARION WILLIAMS

A POEM

" These people have no curtain,"
    Said gentle Ivy Green,
" I'll cover up their window
    So that they can't be seen."
So she dropped swaying branches
    Like portieres from above
With small green leaves all beaded
    As a token of her love.
But when I came and saw it,
    I did not understand,
I tore away the curtain
    With quick and ruthless hand.
Said I, " You naughty hobo,
    Why, this is where I live!
Don't peep into my window!
    You're too inquisitive."
Then all the leaves, aquiver
    With the breezes from the lake,
'Gan sighing, all heart broken
    And I saw my mistake.
I can't bear Ivy's sadness,
    My heart feels every moan,
I'd love the dainty curtain,
    But how can I atone?
This story has a moral;
    Don't cause a heart to bleed,
Because, perhaps, you do not know
    The motive for its deed.

               KATHRYN MARIE RAMBO

CELESTIAL FOOD

A cloth of blue is the sky tonight
And crystal are the stars
The dipper serves a cooling draught
Right from the Milky Way
And other food is there to see. . . .
My hunger grows apace.
The bright new moon is a slice of golden mellon at my place!

CECELIA SLAWIK LAMB

❖　❖　❖

Grievous words should not be spoken
For oh the hearts that they have broken.
Far too often it has been the heart of him who did the sin.
Oh would indeed there were a way
To seal our lips before they say
Those words of bitterness.

SUZANNE LEHMAN

❖　❖　❖

THE DEAD PUSSYCAT

You's stiff an' cold as a stone,
　　Little cat.
Deys done frow'd out an' left you alone,
　　Little cat.
I'se a-strokin' your fur
But you don't never purr,
Nor hump anywhur
　　How is dat, little cat,
　Is you humpn' and purrin' up done?

[82]

Why fer is you little tail tied,
  Little cat?
Did dey pizen you tumick inside,
  Little cat?
Did dey pound you wif bricks,
Or wif big nasty sticks,
Or abuse you wif kicks,
  Little cat, tell me dat.
Did dey holler whenever you cried?

Did it hurt very bad when you died
  Little cat?
Why didn't you run off an' hide,
  Little cat?
I'se wet in my eyes,
When a little cat dies,
  Little cat, think of dat.
An' I'se awfully sorry, besides.

Dest lay still there down in the gwoun,
  Little cat.
While I tucks de gween gwass awoun,
  Little cat.
Dey can't hurt you no more,
When you's tired an' sore,
Dest keep quiet, you pore
  Little cat, wif a pat,
An' forget all de kicks of de town.

❖ ❖ ❖

THE LOST PUPPY

Say! little Pup,
            What's up?
Your tail is down
And out of sight,

Between your legs;
    Why, that aint right.
        Little Pup,
            Brace up!

Say! little Pup,
            Look up!
Don't hang your head
And look so sad,
You're all mussed up,
But you aint mad.
        Little Pup,
            Cheer up!

Say! little Pup,
            Stir up!
Is that a string
Around your tail?
And was it fast
    To a tin pail?
        Little Pup,
            Git up!

Say! little Pup,
            Talk up!
Were those bad boys
All after you
With sticks and stones,
    And tin-cans, too.
        Little Pup,
            Speak up!

Say! little Pup,
Stand up!
Let's look at you;
You'd be all right

If you was scrubbed
    And shined up bright.
    Little Pup,
        Jum Up!

Say! little Pup,
        Bark up!
Let's hear your voice.
Say, you're a brick!
Now, try to beg
And do a trick.
    Little Pup,
        Sit up!

Say! little Pup,
        Chime up!
Why, you can sing —
Now, come with me;
Let's wash and eat
And then we'll see,
    Little Pup,
        What's up!

HENRY FIRTH WOOD

❖ ❖ ❖

MY DOG

I have a little puppy,
Just an ugly little hound,
His coat's as homely as can be,
His tail most reaches ground.
His paws are twice too big for him,
And you can plainly see
He ain't no special breed at all,
But he's all right for me.

He dug down underneath our porch
A hole as deep could be
And dragged a few things in there,
I'll name them so you'll see,
A pillow case, Ma's false hair switch,
And then our old door mat,
A rubber, and Pa's best pair of shoes
And Sis's beau's good hat.

He teases the cat most awful,
It's dandy fun to see,
For every bite she gives him
He yelps and gives her three.
He's just one dandy dog,
This little pup of mine
And for all my Ma may say
I sure do like him fine.

Ma says, " Oh give him away,"
And screams when he comes round.
Pa says, " Oh let him stay,"
My Pa he likes that hound.
So stay he will, this little pup
And grow right up with me.
And he goes where I go
'Cause he's my Pal, you see.

MABEL JOYCE

❖   ❖   ❖

NEXT DOOR DOG

Some people say the next door dog
And mine are just the same.
They say the only difference is
Mine has a different name.

They say that tail and spot and ears
And eyes and nose and bark
Are just the same as my dog
In the daylight or the dark.
But for a million dollars down
And fifty million more
I wouldn't trade my little dog
For the little dog next door.
He may look just the same to you
And he may be just as fine
BUT —
The next door dog is the next door dog
And mine — is — Mine.

DIXIE WILLSON

❖   ❖   ❖

THE TALE OF A MOUSE

As recited by Elizabeth Brogden Stanistreet in 1854 in Thorn Hill
Leeds, Yorkshire, England.

In a crack near the cupboard with dainties provided
A certain young mouse with her mother resided.
So securely they lived in that snug quiet spot
Any mouse in the land might have envied their lot.
But one day the young mouse who was given to roam
Having made an excursion one day from her home
On a sudden returned with such joy in her eyes
That her gray sedate parent expressed some surprise.
" Oh mother," said she, " the good folks of this house
I'm convinced have not any ill will to a mouse
And those tales can't be true that you always are telling
For they've been at such pains to construct us a dwelling.
The floor is of wood and the walls are of wires
Exactly the size that one's comfort requires

And the best of all is they've provided as well
With a large piece of cheese of most exquisite smell.
And I near put in my head to go through
When I thought it my duty to come and fetch you."
" Oh child," said her mother, " believe I entreat
Both the cage and the cheese is a most terrible cheat.
Do not think all the trouble they took for our good
For they'd catch us and kill us all if they could
As they've caught and killed scores and please endeavor to
    learn
That a mouse who once enters does never return."

MORAL: Let the young people mind what the old people
      say
      And when danger is near them keep out of the way.

❖ ❖ ❖

KEPT IN

(for Miss Grace)

(Bobby muses at his desk on the injustice of teachers, and possible revenge.)

One of these days
I will really come riding,
On a fiery palfrey with a gliding tail,
And I'll rein in my steed,
Won't I just! And jump off with a rattle of spurs,
And my armor gleaming,
And my helmet streaming with three purple plumes.

I'll draw my sword —
And Teacher'll come running towards me —
And she'll fall on her knees and pray!
(Serve her right) and without looking at her

[88]

I'll march by her — and say!
I'll take my battle-axe and smash these desks up!
And the kids will see the flash of my lance
And they'll come, and thank me, and kiss my hand
And dance —
And I'll just prance off with a kind of expression —
Then it won't matter at all how many apples it takes
To fill a basket that holds three dozen canteloupes.
No! I'd laugh at her if she asked me!
Teacher, is this here answer right?
Whoopee! I'm going! Goodnight!
Hey, Stew! How's the swimmin' today?

MARY CORONA SCHOFF

❖ ❖ ❖

A BOY'S OWN HOUSE

When I get big I'm goin' to have a boy's own kind of house
Where boys won't have to keep themselves as quiet as a
mouse.
In my new house there won't be any doormats at the doors,
Nor any oriental rugs, nor any polished floors.
A fellow coming home from play won't have to scrape his
feet,
Or think about his muddy tracks and keep the carpets
neat.
There'll be a dozen cookie jars upon the pantry shelves
And all a fellow's hungry friends can come and help them-
selves.
I'll hire a baker by the year to keep the cupboard filled
With pie and cake and crullers, in the house I mean to build.

There won't be any stairways in my house, not anywheres;
You'll have to climb a ladder when you want to go upstairs;

[89]

And coming down, you'll do the way the firemen do — just
jump
And wrap your legs around a pole and down you come,
kebump!
I'll put a cross-bar in the hall for hanging by your knees,
And decorate the parlor with an elegant trapeze.
Then out there in the dining-room where now you see the
dome
I'll hang a man-size punching bag to make it seem like
home.
And downstairs in the cellar, I'll get rid of all the coal
And make a splendid alley, where the neighbor boys can
bowl.

I'll have a flashing wireless on the ridge-pole overhead
And talk to all the battleships while lying in my bed;
I'll have a lab'atory, where I'll make things fume and fizz,
And then a forge and workshop too, with every tool there is.
I'll have a billiard table and a fine big handsome court,
And when I build my rifle range, you'll see some famous
sport.
And all my doors will shut themselves — I'll hang them all
on springs —
And every room will need to have a pair of flying rings;
And there won't be any walks to clean when snow begins to
fall —
Good reason why — the house I build won't have any walks
at all.

There'll never be a bath tub in the house I mean to build,
And if a boy forgets to wash he won't get almost killed.
I'll have a swimming tank instead, so deep a boy can dive;
You'll see we'll keep ourselves as clean as any boys alive.
I'll put it where the lib'ry is and give the books away
And line the walls with marble, like the new Y. M. C. A.

There'll be a fine long spring-board and a bully slippery
    slide,
And maybe there will be a raft a-floating on the tide.
And then, there won't be a director to chase us out, I hope,
And you can bet your life on this — there won't be any
    soap!

The men that do the building now, they don't know how
    at all.
They're always sticking windows where a feller might play
    ball.
In all their stupid houses, their apartments and their flats
They never leave a place for dogs or guinea pigs or cats.
When I build mine, I'm going to have a kennel down below,
And pigeons in the attic, and a place upstairs to grow
White rats and mice and Belgian hares; and then I'll have
    some pens
For lizards and canary birds and squirrels and bantam hens.
If architects were ever boys I guess they soon forget,
I'll show them how to build a house when I get big, you bet!

P.S.   The only pictures I'll have in my house will be
    moving pictures.

L. H. R.

❖   ❖   ❖

TEDDY JOE

I've got a darn old, dear old dog.
   His name is Teddy Joe,
And he won't go home when I tell him to,
   And he goes everywhere I go.

He stays with me when I got to work,
   And he goes with me to school,
And he goes in the water along with me
   Down at the swimmin'-pool.

[91]

Sometimes when I fall and hurt myself
    And mother's far away,
Why, Teddy kisses away the tears —
    I ain't a baby, say —

I'm brave, of course, but then sometimes
    A feller's got to cry!
Well, Teddy Joe don't notice it —
    He looks up at the sky.

Jim said he'd give me his white rat
    For dear old Teddy Joe,
But gee! I love that darn old dog,
    I couldn't let him go.

I don't want Eddie's ball and bat,
    I don't want Johnny's frog,
It seems I don't want nothin' but
    My darn old, dear old dog.

KATHRYN MARIE RAMBO

❖ ❖ ❖

A BOY'S SONG

Where the pools are bright and deep,
Where the grey trout lies asleep,
Up the river and over the lea,
That's the way for Billy and me.

Where the blackbird sings the latest,
Where the hawthorne blooms the sweetest,
Where the nestlings chirp and flee,
That's the way for Billy and me.

Where the mowers mow the cleanest,
Where the hay lies thick and greenest,
There to track the homeward bee,
That's the way for Billy and me.

Where the hazel bank is steepest,
Where the shadows fall the deepest,
Where the clustering nuts fall free,
That's the way for Billy and me.

Why the boys should drive away
Little sweet maidens from the play,
Or love to banter and fight so well,
That's the thing I never could tell.

But this I know, I love to play
Through the meadow, among the hay;
Up the water and over the lea,
That's the way for Billy and me.

JAMES HOGG

❖ ❖ ❖

I WISH I HAD A SPOTTED BRONC

I wish I had a spotted bronc
And a gun slung at my side
With a Sears and Roebuck saddle
A million miles I'd ride.

I'd follow the trails of Yellow Stone
I'd travel in Mexico
I'd hit the rodeo in Cheyenne
And a million miles I'd go.

Heaven would furnish a cover
The earth a mattress lend
My pony would be my pardner
And God would be my friend.

ROBERT J. EATON

❖ ❖ ❖

IT AIN'T LATE

Aw gee Ma — I don't want to go to bed,
It ain't late. Why you just said
That Sis was going early to the dance.
Gee, us kids don't get a chance.

Early in the morning and early at night
It always makes me mad enough to fight,
If I don't hear you, I hear Aunt Kate,
" Come now Sonny, it's getting very late."

Gee! us kids don't get a chance.

LUCILLE MURRAY

❖ ❖ ❖

BOY, LIFT YOUR CHIN

Boy, lift your chin
    As you frolic around,
Don't drop your eyes
    To the muck on the ground.
Look straight ahead
    For the dangerous pit
Blocking your path;
    You may fall into it.

Boy, lift your chin
  When temptations allure;
Face daily trials
  With reliance secure.
You can achieve
  Every coveted goal,
If you have faith
  And your actions control.

Boy, lift your chin
  And behold the bright views,
Eyes on the ground
  Only tend to confuse;
Sunshine and sky
  With its beautiful blue;
Beauty and love —
  God arranged them for you.

Boy, lift your chin
  And enjoy every sight;
Keep your steps firm
  And believe right is might.
Let the world see
  You can fight and can smile.
Boy, lift your chin,
  It will help all the while.

EDWIN M. ABBOTT

❖ ❖ ❖

MARCH

March is just a culprit,
A boy with rosy cheek
Always doing something;
But likes to hide and seek,
Mischievous and robust
All the live-long day.

Loves to fuss up little girls
Who've just come out to play.
Likes to whistle, loves to shout
Makes you always live in doubt
As to what the day will be
Like.   The boys cry " Hully Gee,
Gotta wear them mittens yet? "
And March just chuckles
" Burr!   You bet."

GRETTA M. MC OMBER

❖ ❖ ❖

PARENTS

When Ma is sick, she pegs away
She's quiet though, not much to say,
She goes right on a-doin' things
An' sometimes laughs or even sings.
She says she don't feel extra well
But then it's just a kind of spell
She'll be all right tomorrow sure.
A good old sleep will be the cure.
An' Pa he sniffs an' makes no kick
For women folks is always sick,
An' Ma she smiles, lets on she's glad —
When Ma is sick it ain't so bad.

When Pa is sick he's scared to death
An' Ma an' us just hold our breath.
He crawls in bed an' puffs an' grunts
An' does all kind of crazy stunts.
He wants Doc Brown an' mighty quick,
For when Pa's ill he's awful sick!

He gasps an' groans an' sort o' sighs
He talks so queer an' rolls his eyes.
He jumps an' runs an' all of us
An' all the house is in a fuss.
An' peace an' joy is mighty skeerce —
When Pa is ill it's somethin' fierce!

❖   ❖   ❖

LITTLE BILLEE

There were three sailors of Bristol City
  Who took a boat and went to sea.
But first with beef and captain's biscuits
  And pickled pork they loaded she.

There was gorging Jack and guzzling Jimmy,
  And the youngest he was little Billee.
Now when they got as far as the Equator
  They'd nothing left but one split pea.

Says gorging Jack to guzzling Jimmy,
  " I am extremely hungaree."
To gorging Jack says guzzling Jimmy,
  " We've nothing left, us must eat we."

Says gorging Jack to guzzling Jimmy,
  " With one another we shouldn't agree!
There's little Bill, he's young and tender,
  We're old and tough, so let's eat he.

" Oh, Billee, we're going to kill and eat you,
  So undo the button of your chemie."
When Bill received this information
  He used his pocket-handkershie.

" First let me say my catechism,
    Which my poor mammy taught to me."
" Make haste, make haste," says guzzling Jimmy,
    While Jack pulled out his snickershee.

So Billee went up to the main-topgallant mast,
    And down he fell on his bended knee.
He scarce had come to the twelfth commandment
    When up he jumps. " There's land I see:

" Jerusalem and Madagascar,
    And North and South Amerikee:
There's the British flag a-riding at anchor,
    With Admiral Napier, K. C. B."

So when they got aboard the Admiral's
    He hanged fat Jack and flogged Jimmy;
But as for little Bill he made him
    The captain of a Seventy-three!

WILLIAM MAKEPEACE THACKERAY

❖　❖　❖

GRANDMA'S RADIO

Goin' to see my Grandma
    Used to be such heaps of fun;
She never cared about the noise,
    And I could jump and run;
Sometimes I'd chase the kitty
    Just to see how fast she'd go.
But that was all before the days
    Of Grandma's radio.

My Grandma's cookie jar
  Was filled up to the brim.
But now she hasn't time to bake
  Since she's been listening in.
And all I hear is " Hush, hush, hush,
  Don't bother people so."
Can't have a bit of fun since Grandma
  Got a radio.

Once I said to Grandma,
  " Say, what 'cha hearin' now? "
" Hush, hush," she said, " it's recipes;
  They're telling me just how
To bake a pie," and then she wrote it
  In a little book;
Can't see it's done me any good,
  'Cause she don't stop to cook.

My Grandma always listens,
  No matter what she hears,
And sometimes she is full of smiles
  And sometimes full of tears;
One day she listened fast asleep,
  I know 'cause I heard snores;
When she waked up she said " Oh dear
  I've missed the baseball scores! "

So visitin' at Grandma's
  Is not what it used to be;
They even put the kitty now
  Where she can't play with me;
And all that I'm allowed to do
  Is sit and whisper low.
Gee! there's no more fun at Grandma's
  Since she got a radio!

FLORENCE HASCALL BUTLER

CATCHING THE COLT

With forehead star and silver tail,
And three white feet to match,
The gay, half-broken, sorrel colt
Which one of us could catch?

    " I can," said Dick; " I'm good for that; "
He slowly shook his empty hat.
" She'll think its full of corn," said he;
" Stand back, and she will come to me."
Her head the shy, proud creature raised
As 'mid the daisy flowers she grazed;
Then down the hill, across the brook,
Delaying oft, her way she took;
Then changed her pace, and, moving quick,
She hurried on, and came to Dick.
" Ha! Ha! " he cried, " I've caught you, Beck! "
And put the halter around her neck.

But soon there came another day,
    And, eager for a ride —
    " I'll go and catch the colt again:
I can," said Dick with pride.

    So up the stony pasture lane,
And up the hill, he trudged again;
And when he saw the colt, as slow
He shook his old hat to and fro,
" She'll think it's full of corn," he thought,
" And I shall have her quickly caught.
" Beck! Beck! " he called; and at the sound,
The restless beauty looked around,
Then made a quick, impatient turn,
And galloped off among the fern.

[100]

And when beneath a tree she stopped,
And leisurely some clover cropped,
Dick followed after, but in vain;
His hand was just upon her mane,
When off she flew as flies the wind,
And, panting, he pressed on behind.
Down through the brake, the brook across.
O'er bushes, thistles, mounds of moss,
Round and around the place they passed,
Till breathless Dick sank down at last;
There by, provoked, his empty hat, —
" The colt," he said, " remembers that!
There's always trouble from deceit
I'll never try again to cheat! "

MARIAN DOUGLAS

❖ ❖ ❖

THE MAN IN THE MOON

O the man in the Moon has a crick in his back;
  Whee!
    Whimm!
      Ain't you sorry for him?
And a mole on his nose that is purple and black;
And his eyes are so weak that they water and run
If he dares to dream even he looks at the sun, —
So he just dreams of stars as the doctors advise —
  My!
    Eyes!
      But isn't he wise —
To just dream of stars as the doctors advise?

And the Man in the Moon has a boil on his ear —
  Whee!
    Whing!
      What a singular thing!

I know; but these facts are authentic, my dear,
There's a boil on his ear, and a corn on his chin —
He calls it a dimple, — but dimples stick in —
Yet it might be a dimple turned over, you know;
      Whang!
           Ho!
                    Why certainly so! —
It might be a dimple turned over, you know!

And the Man in the Moon has a rheumatic knee —
      Gee!
           Whizz!
                    What a pity that is!
And his toes have worked round where his heels ought to be.
So whenever he wants to go North he goes South,
And comes back with porridge-crumbs all round his mouth,
And he brushes them off with a Japanese fan,
      Whing!
           Whann!
                    What a marvelous man!
What a very remarkably marvelous man!

                          JAMES WHITCOMB RILEY

❖ ❖ ❖

MA'S PHYSICAL CULTURE

Sis takes calisthenics,
Injun clubs an' such,
Reaches f'r her toes ten times
'N' each time makes 'em touch;

Raises up her arms an'
Sweeps 'em all around,
Kicks her heels three times 'ithout
Ever touchin' th' ground.

Ma takes phys'cal culture
In th' washin' tub —
Gets th' clo'es an' soaks 'em down
'N' 'en begins to rub;
Makes ten thousand motions
Up an' down 'at way —
She gets lots o' exercise
In a workin' day!

Sis goes t' th' gym an'
Travels on the rings,
'N' 'en she takes a big, deep breath,
'N' 'en she yells an' sings —
Says it's good f'r weakness
In th' lungs; an' say!
Tennis is her hardest work —
Ought t' see her play!

Ma, she washes dishes,
'N' 'en she sweeps th' floor.
'N' 'en she chops the kindlin'
When her work is through —
Has t' do it, 'cause pa, he's
Calisthenic, too!

Both take phys'cal culture,
But I tell you this:
They's lots o' diff'unce 'tween th' kind
My ma takes, an' Sis!

❖ ❖ ❖

THE HARE WITH MANY FRIENDS

Friendship, like love, is but a name,
Unless to one you stint the flame.
The child whom many fathers share,
Hath seldom known a father's care.

'Tis thus in friendship; who depend
On many, rarely find a friend.
A Hare, who, in a civil way,
Complied with everything, like Gay,
Was known by all the bestial train,
Who haunt the wood, or graze the plain
Her care was, never to offend,
And every creature was her friend.
As forth she went at early dawn,
To taste the dew-besprinkled lawn,
Behind she hears the hunter's cries,
And from the deep-mouthed thunder flies:
She starts, she stops, she pants for breath;
She hears the near advance of death;
She doubles, to mislead the hound,
And measures back her mazy round;
Till, fainting in the public way,
Half dead with fear she gasping lay.
What transport in her bosom grew,
When first the Horse appeared in view!
"Let me," says she, " Your back ascend,
And owe my safety to a friend.
You know my feet betray my flight;
To friendship every burden's light."
The Horse replied: " Poor honest Puss,
It grieves my heart to see thee thus;
Be comforted; relief is near,
For all your friends are in the rear."
She next the stately Bull implored;
And thus replied the mighty lord.
" Since every beast alive can tell
That I sincerely wish you well,
I may, without offence, pretend,
To take the freedom of a friend;
Love calls me hence; a favourite cow

Expects me near yon barley-now:
And when a lady's in the case,
You know, all other things give place.
To leave you thus might seem unkind;
But see, the Goat is just behind."
The Goat remarked her pulse was high,
Her languid head, her heavy eye;
" My back," says he, " may do you harm;
The Sheep's at hand, and wool is warm."
The Sheep was feeble, and complained
His sides a load of wool sustained:
Said he was slow, confessed his fears,
For hounds eat sheep as well as hares.
She now the trotting Calf addressed,
To save from death a friend distressed.
" Shall I," says he, " of tender age,
In this important care engage?
Older and abler passed you by;
How strong are those, how weak am I?
Should I presume to bear you hence,
Those friends of mine may take offence.
Excuse me, then. You know my heart.
But dearest friends, alas! must part!
How shall we all lament: Adieu!
For see, the hounds are just in view."

JOHN GAY

❖   ❖   ❖

PRACTICING TIME

Always whenever I want to play
I've got to practice an hour a day,
Get through breakfast and make my bed,
And Mother says: " Marjorie, run ahead!

There's a time for work and a time for fun,
So, go and get your practicing done."
And Bud, he chuckles and says to me:
" Yes, do your practicing, Marjorie."
A brother's an awful tease, you know,
And he just says that 'cause I hate it so.

They leave me alone in the parlor here
To play the scales or " The Maiden's Prayer,"
And if I stop, Mother's bound to call,
" Marjorie dear, you're not playing at all!
Don't waste your time, but keep right on,
Or you'll have to stay when the hour is gone."
Or maybe the maid looks in at me
And says, " You're not playing as I can see.
Just hustle along — I've got work to do
And I can't dust the room until you get through."

Then when I've run over the scales and things
Like " The Fairies Dance," or " The Mountain Springs,"
And my fingers ache and my head is sore,
I find I must sit here a half hour more.
An hour is terribly long, I say,
When you've got to practice and want to play.
So slowly at times has the big hand dropped
That I was sure that the clock had stopped.
But Mother calls down to me: " Don't forget —
A full hour, please. It's not over yet."

Oh, when I get big and have children too,
There's one thing that I will never do —
I won't have brothers to tease the girls
And make them mad when they pull their curls
And laugh at them when they've got to stay
And practice their music an hour a day;

I won't have a maid like the one we've got,
That likes to boss you around a lot;
And I won't have a clock that can go so slow
When it's practice time, 'cause I hate it so!

EDGAR GUEST

❖ ❖ ❖

MISS EDITH HELPS THINGS ALONG

" My sister'll be down in a minute, and says you're to wait,
    if you please;
And says I might stay till she came, if I'd promise her
    never to tease,
Nor speak till you spoke to me first. But that's nonsense;
    for how would you know
What she told me to say, if I didn't?   Don't you really
    and truly think so?

" And then you'd feel strange here alone. And you wouldn't
    know just where to sit;
For that chair isn't strong on its legs, and we never use it a
    bit:
We keep it to match with the sofa; but Jack says it would
    be like you
To flop yourself right down upon it, and knock out the
    very last screw.

" Suppose you try! I won't tell. You're afraid to! Oh!
    you're afraid they would think it was mean!
Well, then, there's the album: that's pretty, if you're sure
    that your fingers are clean.
For sister says sometimes I daub it; but she only says that
    when she's cross.
There's her picture. You know it? It's like her; but she
    ain't as good-looking of course.

[107]

" This is ME. It's the best of 'em all. Now, tell me,
    you'd never have thought
That once I was little as that? It's the only one that
    could be bought;
For that was the message to pa from the photograph-man
    where I sat, —
That he wouldn't print off any more till he first got his
    money for that.

" What? Maybe you're tired of waiting. Why, often she's
    longer than this.
There's all her back hair to do up, and all of her front
    curls to friz.
But it's nice to be sitting here talking like grown people,
    just you and me!
Do you think you'll be coming here often? Oh, do! But
    don't come like Tom Lee.

" Tom Lee, her last beau. Why, my goodness! he used to
    be here day and night
Till the folks thought he'd be her husband; and Jack says
    that gave him a fright.
You won't run away then, as he did? for you're not a rich
    man, they say,
Pa says you're poor as a church-mouse. Now, are you?
    and how poor are they?

" Ain't you glad that you met me? Well, I am; for I
    know now your hair isn't red;
But what there is left of it's mousy, and not what that
    naughty Jack said.
But there! I must go: sister's coming! But I wish I could
    wait, just to see
If she ran up to you, and kissed you in the way she kissed
    Mr. Lee.

                                                    BRET HARTE
    [108]

THE ENCHANTED SHIRT

The King was sick. His cheek was red,
  And his eye was clear and bright;
He ate and drank with a kingly zest,
  And peacefully snored at night.

But he said he was sick — and a king should know;
  And doctors came by the score —
They did not cure him. He cut off their heads,
  And sent to the schools for more.

At last two famous doctors came,
  And one was poor as a rat;
He had passed his life in studious toils
  And never found time to grow fat.

The other had never looked in a book;
  His patients gave him no trouble;
If they recovered, they paid him well,
  If they died, their heirs paid double.

Together they looked at the royal tongue,
  As the king on his couch reclined;
In succession they thumped his august chest,
  But no trace of disease could find.

The old sage said, " You're as sound as a nut."
  " Hang him up! " roared the king in a gale —
In a ten-knot gale of royal rage;
  The other leech grew a shadow pale.

But he pensively rubbed his sagacious nose,
  And thus his prescription ran;
" The king will be well if he sleeps one night
  In the shirt of a Happy Man."

Wide o'er the realm the couriers rode,
   And fast their horses ran,
And many they saw, and to many they spake
   But they found no Happy Man.

They found poor men who would fain be rich,
   And rich who thought they were poor;
And men who twisted their waists in stays,
   And women who short hose wore.

They saw two men by the roadside sit,
   And both bemoaned their lot;
For one had buried his wife, he said,
   And the other one had not.

At last they came to a village gate;
   A beggar lay whistling there;
He whistled and sang and laughed, and rolled
   On the grass in the soft June air.

The weary couriers paused and looked
   At the scamp so blithe and gay,
And one of them said, " Heaven save you, friend,
   You seem to be happy today."

" O yes, fair sirs," the rascal laughed,
   And his voice rang free and glad;
" An idle man has so much to do
   That he never has time to be sad."

" This is our man," the courier said,
   " Our luck has led us aright.
I will give you a hundred ducats, friend,
   For the loan of your shirt tonight."

The merry blackguard lay back on the grass
  And laughed till his face was black;
" I would do it, God wot," and he roared with fun,
  " But I haven't a shirt to my back."

Each day to the king the reports came in
  Of his unsuccessful spies,
And the sad panorama of human woes
  Passed daily under his eyes.

And he grew ashamed of his useless life,
  And his maladies hatched in gloom;
He opened the windows, and let in the air
  Of the free heaven into his room.

And out he went in the world and toiled
  In his own appointed way,
And the people blessed him, the land was glad,
  And the king was well and gay.

JOHN HAY

❖ ❖ ❖

INDIAN LEGEND

(*This is a true Indian tale*)

Kookooscoose, the small Indian boy
Ran into his father's teepee
" Please tell me about old Cupkawis
Oh Maka, my mother," cried he.

" Come sit with me close by the fire
So that you will not be cold
And again I will tell you the story
Which often before you've heard told.

[111]

" Cupkawis the very wise owl
And Molsoon the wolf once did plan
How as partners the two might contrive
To rule all who lived on the land.

" ' Come to my lodge, oh you wise one,'
Molsoon the wolf once did say,
' There we will feast by my fire
And carefully our plans we will lay.'

" At his tepee they then held their council
But Cupkawis got nothing to eat
Greedy Molsoon himself cooked the meal
And himself he ate up all the meat.

" Cupkawis arose in great rage,
' Tomorrow I'll show you,' cried he,
' The way that a friend should be treated
When at council within your tepee.'

" Next day when he came to the lodge
Molsoon smiled as he entered the door
Cupkawis for him had prepared
Such a feast as he'd ne'er seen before.

" On the fire were three pots of corn pudding
All cooked with the sweet of the great maple tree,
Mitches the partridge, Maktoques the hare
Were all roasted as fine as could be.

" Near the fire a great kettle of soup
Had been set so that it would stay hot
And of honey the owl had collected
Enough so it filled a large pot.

[112]

" ' Come into my lodge, oh my brother,'
Cupkawis then welcomed his guest.
' Of this feast I will take but a small bowl of soup
You are welcome to all of the rest.'

" Greedy Molsoon began on the soup
Next Maktoques and Mitches ate he
Then followed the pudding and honey
Till no more of the feast could he see.

" Then Molsoon arose in great rage,
' Bring me something to eat now,' cried he,
' You said you would show me the way that a friend
Should be treated within your tepee.'

" ' Here is all that is left in my wigwam,'
Most gallantly answered Cupkawis
' The small bowl of soup which I saved for myself
If you hunger you're welcome to this.'

" Molsoon then quickly emptied the bowl
And leaping again to his feet
He cried, ' Hurry, prepare me a meal
For I have had nothing to eat.'

" Then spake old Cupkawis with scorn,
' Truly you're called selfish one —
I suppose you will want to eat me
Before your repast will be done.'

" Angry Molsoon leaped over the fire
He let forth a bloodthirsty howl
And snatching him feathers and all
He swallowed the peaceful old owl.

"So Cupkawis the owl and sly Molsoon the wolf
Never got to rule much of our land
Because Molsoon the selfish ate up his good friend
And that broke up the partnership planned."

ROBERT J. EATON

❖ ❖ ❖

ALIBI

I hate to go to bed at night
So to stay up, I always fight,
But gee it's hard though they say it pays,
To have to get up on real cold days.

Mother always tells me, and she makes me squirm,
"It's only the early bird catches the worm."
I think I'll tell her when it's cold
And I'm still in my bed,
That I don't like worms anyway
And cover up my head.

ANNE V. KELLY

❖ ❖ ❖

HAVE YOU?

"Have you ever seen an elephant?"
A lady asked one day.
And Jerry who was questioned said,
With shrug of shoulder, "Say,
I lived in Noo York all me life,
I been to Central Park.
The kangaroo's a friend of mine,
The seal, I knows his bark.
Say Lady, the rhinocerous that
Lives up at the Zoo,
To make him jump and holler
All's I gotta say is ' Boo! ' "

" Then you know all of the animals? "
" You bet I do — and how!
You bet I knows dem wild ones
But — I never seen a cow! "

GRETTA M. MC OMBER

❖ ❖ ❖

DO YOU

When you go walking down the street
Do you keep looking at your feet
When there are lots of things to see?
      Hump, not me!

See that little bit of sky?
You have to look away up high
Think such things go right past me?
      Hump, not me!

I like to see the growin' leaves
I like to smile whatever grieves
Think a frown could live with me?
      Hump, not me!

When I think of kids that smile
They beat the others by a mile
I don't think I'd like to be
Like those people who don't see —
      Hump, not me!

WILMOT SCHOFF

THE BAPTIST PARSONAGE

We've moved into the country an' I think we're moved to
    stay,
Though Ma goes to the city almost every other day.
And Sis don't have much time at home; just now she's all
    the rage.
We got a dandy place to live; it's the Baptist parsonage.

Our fam'ly's Presbyterian; Pa says the Baptists don't care
S'long as we pay our rent on time we'll keep on livin' there.
It's a funny house to live in, jes' full of rooms an' doors;
It needs both paint an' paper an' Ma says it needs new
    floors.

The lawn runs all around the house; there isn't much grass
    grows
But Pa gets out his lawn mower an' mows an' mows and
    mows.
An' when it comes to sprinkling Ma says it's waste; an'
    still
Pa says the Baptists won't complain about a water bill.

I've got a room all to myself an' when I'm there it seems
I hear the queerest noises an' dream the queerest dreams.
Last night I dreamed of Noah; an' the fame that came to
    him
An' wondered if he ever learned those boys of his to swim.

Maybe a real great sermon came into a preacher's head,
While in my room a-thinking, at least so my father said.
I've tried to write a sermon — I'd like to learn the art
But gee! I always go to sleep; can't even get a start.

I wonder would we have to move, now that we're settled
    down,
If the church should lose its pastor an' a new one come to
    town.
If such a thing should come to pass I guess we all would
    rave
'Cause now we're part an' parcel of the Baptist parsonage.

JAMES W. STANISTREET

❖ ❖ ❖

BEDTIME

(To Kenneth)

Just because I'm smaller than the rest of my family
Don't seem to me no reason why they should pick on me.
But ever since I can remember when someone of them
    gets cross
They take it out on me 'cause I'm small enough to boss.

Bed ain't such a nice place when you're goin' on nine.
It's awful dark upstairs and I like the firelight fine.
But always just at nightfall when the neighbor ladies come
To tell the folks the gossip, while the shadders scoot an' run,
Mother's sure to raise her eyebrows an' 'fore I can hide has
    said,
" Now William, say your prayers and run along to bed."

Then every Wednesday night sure as ever fate can tell
That awful Henry Scribbens comes to visit my sister Belle!
Belle may be growed up young lady with her hair on top of
    her head
But she can't tell me I gotta say my prayers an' go to bed!

[117]

Bet I never get a chance to get in Heaven to stay
For while I'm waitin' outside the gates watchin' all the
    angels play
An' I see the gang marchin' in the percession I should've
    lead —
Saint Peter'll make me stay outside and say my prayers —
    gosh darn it an' go to bed!

CAROL FLORENCE DERBY

❖ ❖ ❖

THE SUGAR PLUM TREE

Have you ever heard of the sugar-plum tree?
'Tis a marvel of great renown!
It blooms on the shore of the Lollipop sea
In the garden of Shut-Eye town;
The fruit that it bears is so wondrously sweet
(As those who have tasted it say)
That good little children have only to eat
Of that fruit to be happy next day.

When you've got to that tree you would have a hard time
To capture the fruit which I sing:
The tree is so tall that no person could climb
To the bowers where the sugar plums swing.
But up in that tree sits a chocolate cat,
And a gingerbread dog prowls below —
And this is the way you contrive to get at
Those sugar plums tempting you so.

You say but the word to that gingerbread dog,
And he barks with such terrible zest
That the chocolate cat is at once all agog,
As her swelling proportions attest.

[118]

That the chocolate cat goes cavorting around
From this leafy limb unto that,
And the sugar plums tumble, of course, to the ground —
Hurrah for that chocolate cat!

There are marshmallows, gumdrops, and peppermint canes,
And you carry away of the treasure that rains
As much as your apron can hold.
So come little child, cuddle closer to me
In your dainty white nightcap and gown,
And I'll rock you away to that sugar-plum tree
In the garden of Shut-Eye town.

EUGENE FIELD

❖ ❖ ❖

BLINDNESS

When I was young as you may be
I thought someday I would not see.
The strange idea possessed my mind
There'd come a time when I'd be blind.

And so I practised in the dark
To find my things, without a spark
Of any kind of helping light,
Really as though I'd lost my sight.

I still can see as well as you,
But this taught me a thing or two.
This thing I learned, 'tis very wrong
Not to put things where they belong.

MARY A. HIPPLE

*POEMS FOR
HIGH SCHOOL STUDENTS*

RIVER LIGHTS

The tall lights
Quiver
Walking
Down the river,
And through the yellow veils
They wear
You see them shiver.

ISAAC BENJAMIN

❖ ❖ ❖

NOCTURNE

There is a dampness in the air
The Lady of the Pool of Blackness
Has bathed again and has flung
Her ebony hair over the world to dry.

The moon broke through the Lady's hair
Disclosing a sleeping town
That lay like a babe in the arms of a Madonna.

FRANK ANKENBRAND JR.

❖ ❖ ❖

FOR A CRIPPLED GIRL

Are you not beautiful, though aid
But slightly lessens pain?
Your eyes have all the glow in them
Of sun through April rain,
For hope has sunk such vital roots
Deep in your doubting heart
You will not take the truth at once
Apparent on your chart.

Dear child, let not your loveliness
Relinquish hope for grief;
Spring gives to every broken bough
The touch of bud and leaf;
The captive bird who felt the shears
Bite deep across his wings
Forgets the broad blue lanes he flew,
But not the heart that sings.

And when Love comes with hungry eyes
And lips of scarlet flame,
He will not stoop to question why,
Or hesitate in shame;
But in his quick impulsive heart
Your loveliness will burn
So deeply that your hurt becomes
Only his dear concern.

ISAAC BENJAMIN

PRAYER

Not for a long while, O Sun anointed Lord
Do I beseech Thee life; the space of song
Is time enough to make the weary strong,
And then it matters not who wields Thy sword.

Not for old splendours, star illumined Lord
Do I beseech Thee, but that I might pray
For friends Thou gavest me, and friends repay
Kind deed by deed and shining word by word.

ISAAC BENJAMIN

AT MORNING

Another day of life begun,
Another day of toil or fun,
Another day to do a deed
Of kindness to a friend in need;
Another day wherein to share
Our joys, and other people's care;
A day in which some task we do
May bring us friends forever true.

So open wide your eyes, my friend;
Each day you'll find a chance to lend
A helping hand to one in need.
Just open wide your eyes and read
The book of life that's spread before
Your lonely little cottage door.
Come from within your well pleased self,
Take down your hat from yonder shelf,
Come walk with me, until you can
Just learn to be a friend to man.

ARTHUR SNOVER

❖   ❖   ❖

FANTASY FOR A BEGGAR'S OPERA

The maple and oak tree clad in purple mists
opened their fat money bags and flung
the golden coins from their many hands
into the mist breathing pool half expecting
the three nude birches to dive in the icy waters
for their weird shaped golden coins.

FRANK ANKENBRAND JR.

SYMPTOMS OF THE HEART

(*For Robert*)

Affairs of the heart — so many I've heard
That school-girls' first crushes to me seem absurd.
Pete, Johnny, or Tony — many times I've been told
" He said that he loves me " — the story's so old!

Not that I'm queer: no, no complex at all,
Just as regards boys, I simply don't fall.
But now — (can you beat it) — I have been vamped
By the king of flirtations — of coquettes the champ!

I get such a jolt when his eyes gaze in mine
That my heart bumps my nose, and my breath I can't find.
I never thought that a gold head quite near
And two deep blue eyes could make *me* feel queer!

He's ever so bashful — he says very little
But what he declares to me isn't a riddle.
All the whisp'rings and croonings from him mean full well
That he just adores me, but simply can't tell.

The instant we met he smiled right at me
While the joy which I felt was quite plain to see.
And when in a corner his hand sought for mine
I seemed to have taken a glass of rare wine.

On being in love I've now a new slant
I'll have to confess that I like being vamped
By a boy friend to whom this world is still new
For you see, he is almost — but not quite — aged two.

MARGARET E. BEAL

AN IDYLL

I sit in the great daisy-bed
And dry my tawny hair in the wind,
In the wind that laughs like a gipsy.
I take my comb — a frivolous, ornate affair
And play a quaint little tune
That tells of love out in the West,
Of the rose I treasured
Because he touched it,
Of the little home by the lake in the pines
Vined and gardened in fancy,
Of the poets we might have read,
Of the nights we talked round the fire
Of the day we were lost in the forest,
Of —
My hair is dry.
I must part it in the center
And prepare for that next class in history.

OPAL LOUISE JACKSON

❖ ❖ ❖

POINT OF VIEW

Three cedar trees, old dowagers,
   Bonneted in green,
Corseted and dignified
   In rusty bombazine,
Gossiped of their younger days
   When maiden trees were prim
And would not dare to turn their heads
   To please a breeze's whim,
Criticized a slender birch
   With prude severity,

Who pirouetted in the sun
  Where proper folks could see
Her slim bare ankles flashing white
  And, disapproving, note
That she was dressed in taffeta
  Without a petticoat.

Three scarlet maples up the hill,
  Soubrettes with carmined lips,
Dressed in spangled tarlatan,
  Rouged their finger tips,
Gossiped of their gayeties,
  Shook their hennaed hair,
Wondered if a Puritan
  Were living anywhere
Who wore a somber dress and cloak
  With silver buckled shoes,
And who could never do the things
  That actresses would choose;
Then one espied the slim young birch
  And said in swift surprise:
"I do believe a Puritan
  Is right before our eyes!"

HAZEL HARPER HARRIS

❖ ❖ ❖

THE WIND KNOCKS AT MY WINDOW

The wind knocks at my window,
With a double tap, tap.
The wind knocks at my window —
Again I hear its double rap.

Oh, I will open that window
And I will let the wind in,
And all the room let it circle,
And let it clasp and kiss my skin.

Yes, now I have some company,
For I have let the wind inside!
And now I will close that window,
So that the wind may here abide.

LEO KONOPKA

❖ ❖ ❖

A MUSICAL INSTRUMENT

What was he doing, the great god Pan,
    Down in the reeds by the river?
Spreading ruin and scattering ban,
Splashing and paddling with hoofs of a goat,
And breaking the golden lilies afloat
    With the dragon-fly on the river.

He tore out a reed, the great god Pan,
    From the deep cool bed of the river;
The limpid water turbidly ran,
And the broken lilies a-dying lay,
And the dragon-fly had fled away,
    Ere he brought it out of the river.

High on the shore sat the great god Pan,
    While turbidly flowed the river;
And hack'd and hew'd as a great god can
With his hard bleak steel at the patient reed,
Till there was not a sign of the leaf indeed
    To prove it fresh from the river.

He cut it short, did the great god Pan
   (How tall it stood in the river),
Then drew the pith, like the heart of a man,
Steadily from the outside ring,
And notched the poor dry empty thing
   In holes, as he sat by the river.

" This is the way," laugh'd the great god Pan
   (Laugh'd while he sat by the river),
" The only way, since gods began
To make sweet music, they could succeed."
Then dropping his mouth to a hole in the reed,
   He blew in power by the river.

Sweet, sweet, sweet, O Pan!
   Piercing sweet by the river!
Blinding sweet, O great god Pan!
The sun on the hill forgot to die,
And the lilies revived, and the dragon-fly
   Came back to dream on the river.

Yet half a beast is the great god Pan,
   To laugh as he sits by the river,
Making a Poet out of man;
The true gods sigh for the cost and pain —
For the reed which grows nevermore again
   As a reed with the reeds of the river.

ELIZABETH BARRETT BROWNING

❖ ❖ ❖

CAPTIVES

Lock a blackbird in a cage,
Shut a minnow in a bowl —
Yet your captives shall escape;
For their death shall be your toll.

LEO KONOPKA

ROBIN HOOD'S DEATH AND BURIAL

When Robin Hood and Little John
　　Went o'er yon bank of broom,
Said Robin Hood to Little John,
　　" We have shot for many a pound;

" But I am not able to shoot one shot more, —
　　My arrows will not flee;
But I have a cousin lives down below,
　　Please God, she will bleed me."

Now Robin is to fair Kirkley gone,
　　As fast as he can win;
But before he came there, as we do hear,
　　He was taken very ill.

And when he came to fair Kirkley Hall,
　　He knocked all at the ring,
But none was so ready as his cousin herself
　　For to let bold Robin in.

" Will you please sit down, Cousin Robin," she said,
　　" And drink some beer with me? " —
" No, I will neither eat nor drink
　　Till I am blooded by thee."

" Well, I have a room, Cousin Robin," she said
　　" Which you did never see,
And if you please to walk therein,
　　You blooded by me shall be."

She took him by the lily-white hand,
　　And led him to a private room,
And there she blooded bold Robin Hood
　　Whilst one drop of blood would run.

She blooded him in the vein of the arm,
And locked him up in the room;
There he did bleed all the livelong day,
    Until the next day at noon.

He then bethought him of a casement door,
    Thinking for to be gone;
He was so weak he could not leap,
    And he could not get down.

He then bethought him of his bugle-horn,
    Which hung low down to his knee;
He set his horn unto his mouth,
    And blew out weak blasts three.

Then Little John when hearing him,
    As he sat under the tree,
" I fear my master is near dead,
    He blows so wearilee."

Then Little John to fair Kirkley is gone,
    As fast as he can flee;
But when he came to Kirkley Hall,
    He broke locks two or three;

Until he came bold Robin to,
    Then he fell on his knee;
" A boon, a boon," cries Little John,
    " Master, I beg of thee."

" What is that boon," quoth Robin Hood,
    " Little John, thou begst of me? " —
" It is to burn fair Kirkley Hall,
    And all their nunnerie."

"Now nay, now nay," quoth Robin Hood,
  "That boon I'll not grant thee;
I never hurt woman in all my life,
  Nor man in woman's companie.

"I never hurt fair maid in all my time,
  Nor at my end shall it be.
But give me my bent bow in my hand,
  And a broad arrow I'll let flee,

"And where this arrow is taken up,
  There shall my grave digged be.
Lay me a green sod under my head,
  And a broad arrow I'll let flee,

"And lay my bent bow by my side,
  Which was my music sweet;
And make my grave of gravel and green,
  Which is most right and meet.

"Let me have length and breadth enough,
  With a green sod under my head,
That they may say, when I am dead,
  Here lies bold Robin Hood."

These words they readily promised him,
  Which did bold Robin Hood please;
And there they buried bold Robin Hood,
  Near to the fair Kirkleys.

OLD BALLAD

THE LASSIE OF "YEARS AGO"

When I sail down the beautiful River of Thought
   Over Memory's silver Sea,
I meet in the Land of Years Ago
   The lassie that once was me.

I smile at the two little braids of hair
   And the turned-up, freckled nose,
But when I was just a little lass
   I cried over both of those.

I harbored a dream of golden curls
   And a skin like the driven snow,
But I really do not want them now
   When I visit " Long Ago."

For there, far away in the " Long Ago,"
   When that lassie laughs so free,
And I see her curl up in mother's arms
   I wish — that she still were me.

And I'm sure, if for one dear, glorious day
   I could be again just eight,
My whole future life would better be
   For that dear little lassie's sake.

                      KATHRYN MARIE RAMBO

❖ ❖ ❖

THE QUEER ONE

He was a queer one. Sometimes all day long
   He'd lie there watching clouds from in the grass;
He said it seemed like God's parade
   To see them pass.

He'd go out picking weeds, tansy and dock,
    Yarrow, horse-sorrel — things like those, for hours,
When all his yard was running over full
    With proper flowers.

Funny the way he went!   One winter night
    We went out looking — he'd been gone since noon —
And found him lying in a field, his eyes
    Set on the moon.

We thought he was alive — his coat just moved —
    So someone laid it back a little way
To feel his heart, but where it should have beat
    A field-mouse lay.

RHEA DE CONDRES

❖   ❖   ❖

CHI LIEN CHANG

Chi Lien Chang
Was a wise and worthy noble,
Who understood the Great Tao,
And was favored by the Dragon.
When the Son of Heaven lay dead
Among the Dragon-broidered robes
In the bed of yellow gold
In the purple palace,
The Mandarins came to Chi Lien Chang,
And their leader whispered in his ear:
" Come and be our Emperor —
Son of Heaven,
Live in the purple palace,
Sleep in the bed of yellow gold,
With the Dragon-broidered robes."
But Chi Lien Chang was pained,

[135]

As if he heard ill news;
With all due formality he refused.
When the Mandarins had gone
Back to the purple palace,
Chi Lien Chang went down to the pool,
And dipped water, cool and clear,
From among the frogs and lotus,
And washed out his ear.

HERMAN LIVEZEY

❖ ❖ ❖

IMMORTALITY

Like a head with streaming golden hair
Does each comet blaze across the sky;
Though it disappears forevermore,
Still it blazes elsewhere — cannot die. . . .

LEO KONOPKA

❖ ❖ ❖

SONG OF A SMILING LADY

I used to fear lest man might probe
The tear-pools in my heart,
Or woman's deft and delicate touch
Old wounds should stretch apart;
But now I walk serenely on
Past every fool and knave,
For I have found a little smile
Will serve me like a slave.

I'll wear a ribbon in my hair,
A jewel at my throat —
And when I shiver, I'll put on
A very crimson coat.

No one shall know I'm weary,
Nor wonder why I'm grave,
For I have found a little smile
Will serve me like a slave.

And the fortune others think I own
Prodigally I can give;
I'll cheer them like a singing bird
The longest day I live.
White roses for a happy maid
They'll strew upon my grave —
And all because that little smile
Still served me like a slave!

KATHERINE BREGY

❖　❖　❖

AUNT TABITHA

Whatever I do, and whatever I say,
Aunt Tabitha tells me that isn't the way:
When she was a girl (forty summers ago)
Aunt Tabitha tells me they never did so.

Dear Aunt! if I only would take her advice!
But I like my own way and I find it so nice!
And besides, I forget half the things I am told —
But they all will come back to me when I am old.

If a youth passes by, it may happen no doubt,
He may chance to look in as I chance to look out —
She would never endure an impertinent stare;
It is horrid she says and I mustn't sit there.

A walk in the moonlight has pleasure I own;
But it isn't quite safe to be walking alone —
So I take a lad's arm, just for safety, you know,
But Aunt Tabitha tells me she never did so.

How wicked we are — and how good they were then!
They kept at arm's length those detestable men.
What an era of virtue she lived in! but stay —
Were the men all such rogues in Aunt Tabitha's day?

If the men were so wicked, I'll ask my papa
How he dared to propose to my darling mamma?
Was he like the rest of them? Goodness! who knows?
And what should I do if a wretch should propose?

I am thinking if Aunt knew so little of sin,
What a wonder Aunt Tabitha's aunt must have been!
And her grand-aunt! It scares me! How shockingly sad
That the girls of today are so frightfully bad!

A martyr will save us — and nothing else can!
Let me perish to rescue some wretched young man.
Though when to the altar a victim I go,
Aunt Tabitha'll tell me she never did so!

OLIVER WENDELL HOLMES

❖　❖　❖

LUCY GRAY

Oft have I heard of Lucy Gray;
　And, when I crossed the wild,
I chanced to see, at break of day,
　The solitary child.

No mate, no comrade, Lucy knew;
　She dwelt on a wide moor,
The sweetest thing that ever grew
　Beside a human door.

"Tonight will be a stormy night,
    You to the town must go;
And take a lantern, child, to light
    Your mother through the snow."

"That, Father, will I gladly do;
    'Tis scarcely afternoon,
The minster clock has just struck two,
    And yonder is the moon."

At this the father raised his hook
    And snapped a faggot band;
He plied his work; and Lucy took
    The lantern in her hand.

Not blither is the mountain roe;
    With many a wanton stroke
Her feet disperse the powdery snow,
    That rises up like smoke.

The storm came on before its time;
    She wandered up and down,
And many a hill did Lucy climb,
    But never reached the town.

The wretched parents all that night
    Went shouting far and wide;
But there was neither sound nor sight
    To serve them for a guide.

At daybreak on a hill they stood
    That overlooked the moor,
And thence they saw the bridge of wood,
    A furlong from their door.

You yet may spy the fawn at play,
  The hare upon the green;
But the sweet face of Lucy Gray
  Will never more be seen.

And, turning homeward, now they cried,
  " In heaven we all shall meet! "
When in the snow the mother spied
  The print of Lucy's feet.

Then downward from the steep hill's edge
  They tracked the footmarks small,
And through the broken hawthorn hedge
  And by the long stone wall:

And then an open field they crossed;
  The marks were still the same;
They tracked them on, nor ever lost;
  And to the bridge they came.

They followed from the snowy bank
  The footmarks one by one,
Into the middle of the plank;
  And farther were there none!

Yet some maintain that to this day
  She is a living child,
That you may see sweet Lucy Gray
  Upon the lonesome wild.

O'er rough and smooth she trips along,
  And never looks behind,
And sings a solitary song
  That whistles in the wind.

WILLIAM WORDSWORTH

KENTUCKY BELLE

Summer of 'sixty-three, sir, and Conrad was gone away —
Gone to the county-town, sir, to sell our first load of hay —
We lived in the log-house yonder, poor as ever you've seen;
Roschen there was a baby, and I was only nineteen.

Conrad, he took the oxen, but he left Kentucky Belle;
How much we thought of Kentuck, I couldn't begin to
    tell —
Came from the Blue-Grass country; my father gave her
    to me
When I rode North with Conrad, away from the Tennessee.

Conrad lived in Ohio — a German he is, you know —
The house stood in broad corn-fields, stretching on, row
    after row:
The old folks made me welcome; they were kind as kind
    could be;
But I kept longing, longing, for the hills of the Tennessee.

O, for a sight of water, the shadowed slope of a hill!
Clouds that hang on the summit, a wind that never is still!
But the level land went stretching away to meet the sky —
Never a rise, from north to south, to rest the weary eye!

From east to west, no river to shine out under the moon,
Nothing to make a shadow in the yellow afternoon:
Only the breathless sunshine, as I looked out, all forlorn;
Only the " rustle, rustle," as I walked among the corn.

When I fell sick with pining, we didn't wait any more,
But moved away from the corn-lands out to this river
    shore —
The Tuscarawas it's called, sir — off there's a hill, you see —
And now I've grown to like it next best to the Tennessee.

I was at work that morning. Some one came riding like mad
Over the bridge and up the road — Farmer Rouf's little lad:
Bareback he rode; he had no hat; he hardly stopped to say,
" Morgan's men are coming, Frau; they're galloping on this
    way.

" I'm sent to warn the neighbors. He isn't a mile behind;
He sweeps up all the horses — every horse that he can find:
Morgan, Morgan the raider, and Morgan's terrible men,
With bowie-knives and pistols, are galloping up the glen."

The lad rode down the valley, and I stood still at the door;
The baby laughed and prattled, playing with spools on the
    floor;
Kentuck was out in the pasture; Conrad, my man, was gone;
Near, nearer Morgan's men were galloping, galloping on!

Sudden I picked up baby, and ran to the pasture-bar:
" Kentuck! " I called; " Kentucky! " She knew me ever
    so far!
I led her down the gully that turns off there to the right,
And tied her to the bushes; her head was just out of sight.

As I ran back to the log-house, at once there came a sound —
The ring of hoofs, galloping hoofs, trembling over the
    ground —
Coming into the turnpike out from the White-Woman
    Glen —
Morgan, Morgan the raider, and Morgan's terrible men.

As near they drew and nearer, my heart beat fast in alarm;
But still I stood in the doorway, with baby on my arm.
They came; they passed; with spur and whip in haste they
    sped along —
Morgan, Morgan the raider, and his band six hundred
    strong.

Weary they looked and jaded, riding through night and
through day;
Pushing on East to the river, many long miles away,
To the border-strip where Virginia runs up into the West,
And ford the Upper Ohio before they could stop to rest.

On like the wind they hurried, and Morgan rode in advance:
Bright were his eyes like live coals, as he gave me a sideways
glance;
And I was just breathing freely, after my choking pain,
When the last one of the troopers suddenly drew his rein.

Frightened I was to death, sir; I scarce dared look in his
face,
As he asked for a drink of water, and glanced around the
place:
I gave him a cup, and he smiled — 'twas only a boy, you
see;
Faint and worn, with dim blue eyes; and he'd sailed on the
Tennessee.

Only sixteen he was, sir — a fond mother's only son —
Off and away with Morgan before his life had begun!
The damp drops stood on his temples; drawn was the boyish
mouth;
And I thought me of the mother waiting down in the South.

O, pluck was he to the backbone, and clear grit through and
through;
Boasted and bragged like a trooper; but the big words
wouldn't do:
The boy was dying, sir, dying, as plain as plain could be,
Worn out by his ride with Morgan up from the Tennessee.

But, when I told the laddie that I too was from the South,
Water came in his dim eyes, and quivers around his mouth:
" Do you know the Blue-grass country? " he wistful began
    to say;
Then swayed like a willow sapling, and fainted dead away.

I had him into the log-house, and worked and brought him
    to;
I fed him, and coaxed him, as I thought his mother'd do;
And, when the lad got better, and the noise in his head was
    gone,
Morgan's men were miles away, galloping, galloping on.

" O, I must go," he muttered; " I must be up and away!
Morgan, Morgan is waiting for me; O, what will Morgan
    say? "
But I heard a sound of tramping, and kept him back from
    the door —
The ringing sound of horses' hoofs, that I had heard before.

And so, on came the soldiers — the Michigan cavalry —
And fast they rode, and black they looked, galloping rapidly:
They had followed hard on Morgan's track; they had fol-
    lowed day and night;
But of Morgan and Morgan's raiders they had never caught
    a sight.

And rich Ohio sat startled through all those summer days;
For strange, wild men were galloping over her broad high-
    ways;
Now here, now there, now seen, now gone, now north, now
    east, now west,
Through river-valleys and corn-land farms, sweeping away
    her best.

A bold ride and a long ride!   But they were taken at last:
They almost reached the river by galloping hard and
    fast;
But the boys in blue were upon them ere ever they gained
    the ford,
And Morgan, Morgan the raider, laid down his terrible
    sword.

Well, I kept the boy till evening — kept him against his
    will —
But he was too weak to follow, and sat there pale and still:
When it was cool and dusky — you'll wonder to hear me
    tell —
But I stole down to that gully, and brought up Kentucky
    Belle.

I kissed the star on her forehead — my pretty, gentle lass —
But I knew that she'd be happy back in the old Blue-Grass:
A suit of clothes of Conrad's, with all the money I had,
And Kentuck, pretty Kentuck; I gave to the worn-out lad.

I guided him to the southward as well as I knew how:
The boy rode off with many thanks, and many a backward
    bow;
And then the glow it faded, and my heart began to swell,
As down the glen away she went, my lost Kentucky Belle!

When Conrad came in the evening, the moon was shining
    high;
Baby and I were both crying — I couldn't tell him why —
But a battered suit of rebel gray was hanging on the
    wall,
And a thin old horse with drooping head stood in Kentucky's
    stall.

Well, he was kind, and never once said a hard word to me;
He knew I couldn't help it — 'twas all for the Tennessee:
But, after the war was over, just think what came to
    pass —
A letter, sir; and the two were safe back in the old Blue-
    Grass.

The lad had got across the border, riding Kentucky Belle;
And Kentuck she was thriving, and fat, and hearty, and
    well;
He cared for her, and kept her, nor touched her with whip
    or spur:
Ah! we've had many horses, but never a horse like her!

CONSTANCE FENIMORE WOOLSON

❖ ❖ ❖

THE ROMANCE OF THE SWAN'S NEST

Little Ellie sits alone
'Mid the beaches of a meadow
By a stream-side on the grass,
And the trees are showering down
Doubles of their leaves in shadow
On her shining hair and face.

She had thrown her bonnet by,
And her feet she has been dipping
In the shallow water's flow;
Now she holds them nakedly
In her hands, all sleek and dripping,
While she rocketh to and fro.

Little Ellie sits alone,
And the smile she softly uses
Fills the silence like a speech
While she thinks what shall be done,
And the sweetest pleasure chooses
For her future within reach.

Little Ellie in her smile
Chooses — "I will have a lover,
Riding on a steed of steeds:
He shall love me without guile,
And to him I will discover
The swan's nest among the reeds.

"And the steed shall be red-roan,
And the lover shall be noble,
With an eye that takes the breath:
And the lute he plays upon
Shall strike ladies into trouble
As his sword strikes men to death.

"And the steed it shall be shod
All in silver, housed in azure,
And the mane shall swim the wind;
And the hoofs along the sod
Shall flash onward and keep measure,
Till the shepherds look behind.

"But my lover will not prize
All the glory that he rides in,
When he gazes in my face:
He will say, 'O Love, thine eyes
Build the shrine my soul abides in,
And I kneel here for thy grace!'

" Then, ay, then he shall kneel low,
With the red-roan steed anear him,
Which shall seem to understand,
Till I answer, ' Rise and go!
For the world must love and fear him
Whom I gift with heart and hand.'

" Then he will so pale,
I shall feel my own lips tremble
With a yes I must not say,
Nathless maiden-brave, ' Farewell,'
I will utter, and dissemble —
' Light to-morrow with to-day.'

" Then He'll ride among the hills
To the wide world past the river,
There to put away all wrong;
To make straight distorted wills,
And to empty the broad quiver
Which the wicked bear along.

" Three times shall a young foot-page
Swim the stream and climb the mountain
And kneel down beside my feet —
' Lo, my master sends this gage,
Lady, for thy pity's counting!
What wilt thou exchange for it? '

" And the first time, I will send
A white rose bud for a guerdon,
And the second time, a glove;
But the third time — I may bend
From my pride, and answer — ' Pardon
If he comes to take my love.'

"Then the young foot-page will run,
Then my lover will ride faster,
Till he kneeleth at my knee:
' I am a duke's eldest son,
Thousand serfs do call me master,
But, O Love, I love but thee! '

" He will kiss me on the mouth
Then, and lead me as a lover
Through the crowds that praise his deeds
And, when soul-tied by one troth,
Unto him I will discover
That swan's nest among the reeds."

Little Ellie, with her smile
Not yet ended, rose up gayly,
Tied the bonnet, donn'd the shoe,
And went homeward, round a mile,
Just to see, as she did daily,
What more eggs were with the two.

Pushing through the elm-tree copse,
Winding up the stream, light-hearted,
Where the osier pathway leads,
Past the boughs she stoops — and stops.
Lo, the wild swan had deserted,
And a rat had gnaw'd the reeds!

Ellie went home sad and slow.
If she found the lover ever,
With his red-roan steed of steeds,
Sooth I know not; but I know
She could never show him — never,
That swan's nest among the reeds!

ELIZABETH BARRETT BROWNING

THE BALLAD OF THE YOUNG QUEEN

" This throne is so cold," the young queen said —
" And this crown is so heavy — its weight hurts my head.
These women who value and men who stare!
I cannot breathe in this watchful air.

" Your love, Lord, is dear, but my heart yearns to go
Back to my mountains of fire and of snow.
Back to the sound of a summery sea,
Back where my sisters are waiting for me.

" I cannot rest on this throne, Lord," she said,
" And this crown, though all golden, is heavy as lead!
Once in the woods you wove me a crown —
Remember the leaves as you shook them down?

" You hung it with grapes," she smiled as she said,
" Crowns that are living do not hurt the head.
That was the day for the fruit of the vine;
Remember the banter, the laughter, the wine?

" Could you not spare me away for a space?
A while the queen mother might sit in this place.
Into the distance so swiftly I'd ride,
I'd scarcely be gone, Lord, ere I'm back at your side.

" There in my homeland the hills are aglow,
Fire against sunset — snow against snow.
All my heart's asking to see them again —
Peaks rising up to peaks, chain against chain.

" Lord — I entreat thee — permit me to go
Back to the mountains you too once did know.
This crown is so heavy! " she bowed her bright head.
When comes the morning the young queen is dead.

ELEANORE WIDDIS

SHOCK-HEADED CICELY AND THE
TWO BEARS

"O yes! O yes! O yes! ding dong!"
The bellman's voice is loud and strong;
So is his bell: "O yes! ding dong!"

He wears a red coat with golden lace;
See how the people of the place
Come running to hear what the bellman says!

"O yes! Sir Nicholas Hildebrand
Has just returned from the Holy Land,
And freely offers his heart and hand—

"O yes! O yes! O yes! ding dong!"—
All the women hurry along,
Maids and widows, a chattering throng.

"O sir, you are hard to understand!
To whom does he offer his heart and hand?
Explain your meaning, we do command!"

"O yes! ding dong! you shall understand!
O yes! Sir Nicholas Hildebrand
Invites the ladies of this land

"To feast with him in his castle strong
This very day at three. Ding dong!
O yes! O yes! O yes! ding dong!"

Then all the women went off to dress,
Mary, Margaret, Bridget, Bess,
Patty, and more than I can guess.

They powdered their hair with golden dust
And bought new ribbons — they said they must —
But none of them painted, we will trust.

Long before the time arrives,
All the women that could be wives
Are dressed within an inch of their lives.

Meanwhile, Sir Nicholas Hildebrand
Had brought with him from the Holy Land
A couple of bears — oh, that was grand!

He tamed the bears, and they loved him true
Whatever he told them they would do —
Hark! 'tis the town clock striking two!

Among the maidens of low degree
The poorest of all was Cicely —
A shabbier girl could hardly be.

" Oh, I should like to see the feast,
But my frock is old, my shoes are pieced,
My hair is rough! " — (it never was greased).

The clock struck three!   She durst not go!
But she heard the band, and to see the show,
Crept after the people that went in a row.

When Cicely came to the castle gate
The porter exclaimed, " Miss Shaggy-pate,
The hall is full, and you came too late! "

Just then the music made a din,
Flute, and cymbal, and culverin,
And Cicely, with a squeeze, got in!

Oh, what a sight! full fifty score
Of dames that Cicely knew, and more,
Filling the hall from dais to door!

The dresses were like a garden bed,
Green and gold, and blue and red —
Poor Cicely thought of her tossy head!

She heard the singing — she heard the clatter —
Clang of flagon, and clink of platter —
But, oh, the feast was no such matter!

For she saw Sir Nicholas himself,
Raised on a dais just like a shelf,
And fell in love with him — shabby elf!

Her heart beat quick, aside she stept;
Under the tapestry she crept,
Tousling her tossy hair, and wept!

Her cheeks were wet, her eyes were red —
" Who makes that noise? " the ladies said;
" Turn out that girl with the shaggy head! "

Just then there was heard a double roar,
That shook the place, both wall and floor;
Everybody looked to the door.

It was a roar, it was a growl;
The ladies set up a little howl,
And flapped and clucked like frightened fowl.

Sir Hildebrand for silence begs —
In walk the bears on their hinder legs,
Wise as owls, and merry as grigs!

The dark girls tore their hair of sable;
The fair girls hid underneath the table;
Some fainted; to move they were not able.

But most of them could scream and screech —
Sir Nicholas Hildebrand made a speech:
" Order! ladies, I do beseech! "

The bears looked hard at Cicely
Because her hair hung wild and free —
" Related to us, miss, you must be! "

Then Cicely, filling two plates of gold
As full of cherries as they could hold,
Walked up to the bears, and spoke out bold:

" Welcome to you! and to *you* Mr. Bear!
Will you take a chair? will *you* take a chair?
This is an honor, we do declare! "

Sir Hildebrand strode up to see,
Saying, " Who may this maiden be?
Ladies, this is the wife for me! "

Almost before they could understand,
He took up Cicely by the hand,
And danced with her a saraband.

Her hair was rough as a parlour broom,
It swung, it swirled all round the room —
Those ladies were vexed, we may presume.

Sir Nicholas kissed her on the face,
And set her beside him on the dais,
And made her the lady of the place.

[154]

The nuptials soon they did prepare,
With a silver comb for Cicely's hair:
There were bands of music everywhere.

And in that beautiful bridal show
Both the bears were seen to go
Upon their hind legs to and fro!

Now every year on the wedding-day
The boys and girls come out to play,
And scramble for cherries as they may.

With a cheer for this and the other bear,
And a cheer for Sir Nicholas, free and fair,
And a cheer for Cis, of the tossy hair —

With one cheer more (if you will wait)
For every girl with a curly pate
Who keeps her hair in a proper state.

Sing bear's grease! curling-irons to sell!
Sing combs and brushes! sing tortoise-shell!
O yes! ding dong! the crier, the bell!
— Isn't this a pretty tale to tell?

❖ ❖ ❖

THE LADY OF SHALOTT

PART I

On either side the river lie
Long fields of barley and of rye,
That clothe the wold and meet the sky;
And thro' the field the road runs by
    To many-tower'd Camelot;

And up and down the people go,
Gazing where the lilies blow
Round an island there below,
   The island of Shalott.

Willows whiten, aspens quiver,
Little breezes dusk and shiver
Thro' the wave that runs for ever
By the island in the river
   Flowing down to Camelot.
Four gray walls, and four gray towers,
Overlook a space of flowers,
And the silent isle imbowers
   The Lady of Shalott.

By the margin, willow-veil'd,
Slide the heavy barges trail'd
By slow horses; and unhail'd
The shallop flitteth silken-sail'd
   Skimming down to Camelot;
But who hath seen her wave her hand?
Or at casement seen her stand?
Or is she known in all the land,
   The Lady of Shalott?

Only reapers, reaping early
In among the bearded barley,
Hear a song that echoes cheerly
From the river winding clearly,
   Down to towered Camelot;
And by the moon the reaper weary,
Piling sheaves in uplands airy,
Listening, whispers, " 'Tis the fairy
   Lady of Shalott."

PART II

There she weaves by night and day
A magic web with colors gay.
She has heard a whisper say,
A curse is on her if she stay
   To look down to Camelot.
She knows not what the curse may be,
And so she weaveth steadily,
And little other care hath she,
   The Lady of Shalott.

And moving thro' a mirror clear
That hangs before her all the year,
Shadows of the world appear.
There she sees the highway near
   Winding down to Camelot;
There the river eddy whirls,
And there the surly village-churls,
And the red cloaks of market girls,
   Pass onward from Shalott.

Sometimes a troop of damsels glad,
An abbot on an ambling pad,
Sometimes a curly shepherd-lad,
Or long-haired page in crimson clad,
   Goes by to tower'd Camelot;
And sometimes thro' the mirror blue
The knights come riding two and two;
She hath no loyal knight and true,
   The Lady of Shalott.

But in her web she still delights
To weave the mirror's magic sights,
For often thro' the silent nights
A funeral, with plumes and lights,
   And music, went to Camelot;

Or when the moon was overhead,
Came two young lovers lately wed;
"I'm half sick of shadows," said
    The Lady of Shalott.

Part III

A bow-shot from her bower-eaves,
He rode between the barley-sheaves,
The sun came dazzling thro' the leaves,
And flamed upon the brazen greaves
    Of bold Sir Lancelot.
A red-cross knight for ever kneel'd
To a lady in his shield,
That sparkled on the yellow field,
    Beside remote Shalott.

The gemmy bridle glitter'd free,
Like to some branch of stars we see
Hung in the golden Galaxy.
The bridle bells rang merrily
    As he rode down to Camelot;
And from his blazon'd baldric slung
A mighty silver bugle hung,
And as he rode his armour rung,
    Beside remote Shalott.

All in the blue unclouded weather
Thick-jewell'd shone the saddle-leather,
The helmet and the helmet-feather
Burn'd like one burning flame together,
    As he rode down to Camelot.
As often thro' the purple night,
Below the starry clusters bright,
Some bearded meteor, trailing light,
    Moves over still Shalott.

His broad clear brow in sunlight glow'd;
On burnish'd hooves his war-horse trode;
From underneath his helmet flow'd
His coal-black curls as on he rode,
   As he rode down to Camelot.
From the bank and from the river
He flashed into the crystal mirror,
" Tirra lirra," by the river
   Sang Sir Lancelot.

She left the web, she left the loom,
She made three paces thro' the room,
She saw the water-lily bloom,
She saw the helmet and the plume,
   She looked down to Camelot.
Out flew the web and floated wide;
The mirror cracked from side to side;
" The curse is come upon me! " cried
   The Lady of Shalott.

Part IV

In the stormy east-wind straining,
The pale yellow woods were waning,
The broad stream in his banks complaining,
Heavily the low sky raining
   Over tower'd Camelot;
Down she came and found a boat
Beneath a willow left afloat,
And round about the prow she wrote
   The Lady of Shalott.

And down the river's dim expanse —
Like some bold seer in a trance,
Seeing all his own mischance —
With a glassy countenance
   Did she look to Camelot.

And at the closing of the day
She loosed her chain, and down she lay;
The broad stream bore her far away,
   The Lady of Shalott.

Lying, robed in snowy white
That loosely flew to left and right —
The leaves upon her falling light —
Thro' the noises of the night
   She floated down to Camelot;
And as the boat-head wound along
The willowy hills and fields among,
They heard her singing her last song,
   The Lady of Shalott.

Heard a carol, mournful, holy,
Chanted loudly, chanted lowly,
Till her blood was frozen slowly,
And her eyes were darkened wholly,
   Turn'd to tower'd Camelot;
For ere she reach'd upon the tide
The first house by the water-side,
Singing in her song she died,
   The Lady of Shalott.

Under tower and balcony,
By garden-wall and gallery,
A gleaming shape she floated by,
Dead-pale between the houses high,
   Silent into Camelot.
Out on the wharfs they came
Knight and burgher, lord and dame,
And round the prow they read her name,
   The Lady of Shalott.

Who is this? and what is here?
And in the lighted palace near
Died the sound of royal cheer;
And they crossed themselves with fear,
    All the knights of Camelot;
But Lancelot mused a little space;
He said, " She has a lovely face;
God in His mercy lend her grace,
    The Lady of Shalott."

ALFRED TENNYSON

❖   ❖   ❖

POSTPONED

Any one familiar with farm life knows that when the old dog becomes blind, thoughtless and helpless, it is the sad but humane duty of the farmer to put an end to his suffering. It is generally done by taking him out to the woods and shooting him. The new dog soon wins a place for himself but the old one is not forgotten and many a story begins " You remember old Gip — "

Come along, old chap, yer time's 'bout up;
We got another brindle pup;
I 'lows it's tough an' mighty hard,
But a toothless dog's no good on guard;
So trot along right after me,
An' I'll put yeh out o' yer misery.

Now quit yer waggin' that stumpy tail —
We ain't agoin' fer rabbit er quail;
'Sides you couldn't p'int a bird no more,
Yer old and blind an' stiff an' sore,
An' that's why I loaded the gun today —
Yer a-gittin' cross an' in the way.

I been thinkin' it over; taint no fun;
I don't like to do it but it's got to be done;
Got sort of a notion you know too,
The kind of a job we're goin' to do,
Else why would yeh hang back that-a-way?
Yeh ain't ez young ez yeh once was, hey?

Frisky dog in them days, I note,
When yeh nailed the sneak-thief by the throat;
Can't do that now, an' there ain't no need
A-keepin' a dog that don't earn his feed:
So yeh got to make way fer the brindle pup.
Come along, old chap, yer time's 'bout up.

We'll travel along at an easy jog —
'Course, you don't know, bein' only a dog:
But I can mind when you was sprier,
Wakin' us up when the barn caught fire —
It didn't seem possible: yet I know
That was close onto fifteen year ago.

My, but yer hair was long an' thick
When yeh pulled little Sally out o' the crick;
An' it came in handy that night in the storm,
We coddled to keep each other warm.
Purty good dog, I'll admit — but say,
What's the use o' talkin', yeh had yer day.

I'm hopin' the children won't hear the crack,
Er what'll I say when I git back?
They'd be askin' questions, I know their talk,
An' I'd have to lie 'bout a chicken hawk;
— But the sound won't carry beyond this hill.
All done in a minute — don't bark, stand still.

There, that'll do; steady, quit lickin' my hand.
What's wrong with this gun, I can't understand;
I'm jest ez shaky ez I can be —
Must be the agey's the matter with me,
An' that stitch in the back — what! gittin' old, too —
The dinner-bell's ringin' — fer-me — an' you.

CHARLES E. BAER

❖ ❖ ❖

CAESAR RODNEY'S RIDE

Teachers; tell us of Rodney, Rodney of Delaware!
Some of you start and stammer. Others stand mute and
    stare.
Put up your sums and fables. Listen, that you may hear
The gallop of Caesar Rodney with death always riding
    near.

Heat, like a thick black blanket, closely on Byfield lay;
It harried the flesh and spirit of him who waited for day.
His fevered eyes watched the candle that blinked like a far-
    off star —
They looked from a face on which all the grace was hid by a
    cruel scar.

Out of the heat and blackness clamors atrooping came,
Barking of dogs and thunder of knocks on a door's stout
    frame.
Sternly a nurse hissed, " Silence! " and then came a stranger's
    call;
" McKean bids you ride, I will be at your side, Come
    quickly or freedom will fall."

" He'll die on the way," shrilled a servant; but Rodney was
  out of bed.
" Boots, horse and spurs," he commanded, " and the veiling
  to cover my head! "
" Horses are posted to meet you," the voice in the doorway
  said.
" It is well. I am ready." The weak voice was steady. " I
  will vote or you'll bear me there dead."

It's seventy miles to the State House in the city of William
  Penn,
Seventy miles of torture to forward the freedom of men;
For some in Congress are Tories and others too timid to
  dare,
So Rodney must ride that his vote may decide the ballot of
  Delaware.

Neck by neck through old Dover they galloped, and Rodney
  bent low to his task
It was gray in the East when he tarried to cover his face
  with the mask.
A woman screamed at the vision but Rodney was riding
  again,
Though beneath him, the back of his horse was a rack to
  torture the bravest of men.

Great weariness came upon Rodney. He galloped as one
  in a dream;
But lightning-like pains broke his trances as rocks break a
  mountain stream.
Somewhere, in the misty morning, his comrade faltered and
  fell.
Thence rode at his side, with a long, silent stride, a Shape
  that Rodney knew well.

The tropical heat blaze closed round him; the Veiled and the Death side by side.

At inns and by lanes he changed horses, then on with the furious ride.

Weakness at last made him falter. He fed and then slumbered awhile.

But his will was so strong that his rest was not long, for the goal still lay many a mile.

And then he came into the city, the half-Tory town of Penn;

Down Passyunk Road he galloped, past wondering women and men.

His veil streamed, a pennon of freedom, and his limbs hung like bags of sand;

But the horse he bestrode knew the turns of the road and needed no guiding hand.

So, to the State House came Rodney, merely the shell of a man;

There McKean met and bore him as gently as only a sturdy friend can:

Steadied him into the chamber and gloried to hear him declare:

"For the right to be free, and to end Tyranny, I vote 'aye' for fair Delaware!"

You know the rest of the story, you teachers who teach by rote,

How prudent South Carolina announced the change of its vote;

How Pennsylvania also veered around in Freedom's gale;

How the thirteen broke from their necks the yoke, and a nation was born in travail.

[165]

Paint as a noble portrait, Story, Sargent or Chase,
One of the missing Signer. Show us an eager face
Glorified through its veiling, and we will uplift it where
He ended his ride with Death by his side, brave Rodney of
    Delaware.

RICHARD J. BEAMISH

❖ ❖ ❖

THE YARN OF THE "NANCY BELL"

'Twas on the shores that round our coast,
From Deal to Ramsgate span,
That I found alone, on a piece of stone,
An elderly naval man.

His hair was weedy, his beard was long,
And weedy and long was he;
And I heard this wight on the shore, recite,
In a singular minor key: —

"O, I am a cook and a captain bold,
And the mate of the 'Nancy' brig,
And a bo'sun tight, and a midshipmite,
And the crew of the captain's gig."

And he shook his fists and he tore his hair;
Till I really felt afraid,
For I couldn't help thinking the man had been drinking,
And so I simply said: —

" O, elderly man, it's little I know
Of the duties of men of the sea,
And I'll eat my hand if I understand
How you can possibly be

"At once a cook and a captain bold,
And the mate of the 'Nancy' brig,
And a bo'sun tight, and a midshipmite,
And the crew of the captain's gig!"

Then he gave a hitch to his trousers, which
Is a trick all seamen l'arn,
And having got rid of a thumping quid,
He spun this painful yarn: —

" 'Twas in the good ship 'Nancy Bell,'
That we sailed to the Indian Sea,
And there on a reef, we come to grief,
Which has often occurred to me.

"And pretty nigh all o' the crew was drowned,
(There was seventy-seven o' soul);
And only ten of the 'Nancy's' men
Said 'Here' to the muster roll.

"There was me, and the cook, and the captain bold,
And the mate of the 'Nancy' brig,
And a bo'sun tight, and a midshipmite,
And the crew of the captain's gig.

"For a month, we'd neither wittles nor drink,
Till a hungry, we did feel,
So we drawed a lot, and, accordin', shot
The captain for our meal.

"The next lot fell to the 'Nancy's' mate,
And a delicate dish he made;
Then our appetite with the midshipmite,
We seven survivors, stayed.

" And then we murdered the bo'sun tight,
And he much resembled pig;
Then we wittled free, did the cook and me,
On the crew of the captain's gig.

" Then only the cook and me was left,
And the delicate question, ' Which
Of us two goes to the kettle? ' arose,
And we argued it out as sich.

" Fir I loved that cook as a brother, I did,
And the cook he worshiped me;
But we'd both be blowed if we'd either be stowed
In the other chap's hold, you see.

" ' I'll be eat if you dine off me,' says Tom.
' Yes, that,' says I, ' you'll be.
I'm boiled if I die, my friend,' quoth I;
And, ' Exactly so,' quoth he.

" Says he, ' Dear James, to murder me
Were a foolish thing to do,
For don't you see that you can't cook me,
While I can — and will — cook you? '

" So he boils the water, and he takes the salt
And pepper in portions true,
(Which he never forgot,) and some chopped shalot,
And some sage and parsley, too.

" ' Come here,' says he, with a proper pride,
Which his smiling features tell;
' 'Twill soothing be, if I let you see
How extremely nice you'll smell.'

[168]

" And he stirred it round, and round, and round,
And he sniffed at the foaming froth;
When I ups with his heels, and I smothered his squeals
In the scum of the boiling broth.

" And I eat that cook in a week or less,
And as I eating be
The last of his chops, why I almost drops,
For a wessel in sight I see.

" And I never laugh, and I never smile,
And I never lark nor play;
But I sit and croak, and a single joke
I have — which is to say:

" O, I am a cook and a captain bold,
And the mate of the ' Nancy ' brig,
And a bo'sun tight, and a midshipmite,
And the crew of the captain's gig! "

W. S. GILBERT

❖ ❖ ❖

THE FATE OF A CUBAN SPY

This story was written during the Cuban insurrection of 1895–1898.
In January 1896 Captain General Weyler was sent to that unhappy
Island to pursue a policy which produced conditions that horrified the
world. Within a few months out of a population of 1,600,000, 200,000
died of starvation and disease; most of them women and children.

An army of Spaniards in Cuba went into camp for the night.
The General had ordered a rest; on the morrow all must
    fight.

[169]

That day they had taken a prisoner whom the General
ordered tried
In the camp that night by court martial for being a Cuban
spy.

They soon had the horses all watered and then all the men
were well fed
But the prisoner; and all that they would give him was a
single crust of bread.
Sentries were posted 'round the camp to guard it from sudden
attack,
For the scouts reported the Cubans were only a few miles
back.

The officers went to headquarters for the trial would soon
begin,
And when each man had taken his place they ordered the
prisoner in.
The prisoner, a stalwart Cuban, with no sign of fear in his
face
Came with his guards through the doorway, the noblest man
in the place.

Then a witness told how he'd followed the army around like
a tramp,
Living on what he could pick up, and doing odd jobs 'round
the camp.
In this way he gleaned information and sent it back o'er the
line
And kept his commander well informed of their movements
all the time.

A murmur arose 'gainst the prisoner, it came from all sides
of the court,
They taunted him with his helplessness; it seemed to them
great sport.

The prisoner still brave and fearless as yet had not spoken
a word,
When a Captain shouted, " Hang him; shooting's too good
for a cur! "

" Who says I'm a cur? " cried the prisoner; the Captain re-
plied with a sneer,
" I say you're a cur; all Cubans are curs; your hearts are
frozen with fear."
Then the prisoner with strength superhuman struck his
guards in the face.
And madly reached out for the Captain who'd insulted the
Cuban race.

The Captain right quick drew a pistol and aimed at the
prisoners heart;
But his aim was very unsteady and the bullet went wide of
its mark;
Then the Cuban reached up for the pistol and wrenched it
out of his hand
And threw it over the heads of the crowd through the doorway into the sand.

Then turning again to his judges he said, " We'll fight without that and see
Which of the two is the greatest cur; this cowardly Captain
or me."
The Captain, a big burly Spaniard with muscles as hard as
a stone,
Looked down on the stalwart Cuban and treachery from his
eyes shone.

As he took his position for fighting, " I'll save you the
trouble," he said,
" Of hanging this cur in the morning; I'll kill him or die in
his stead! "

Then the fighting began in earnest; not a soul in the tent
    dared move
First the Cuban was down; then the Spaniard the Cuban's
    eyes glaring above.

But the Spaniard is up in a moment, a knife in his hand like
    a flash,
He rushed for the gallant young Cuban, his arm in position
    to slash,
But the Cuban is ready and waiting, his eyes all aglow with
    fire,
And catching hold of the Spaniards arm he twisted it just
    like wire.

And then with the strength of a Samson he lifted him from
    the ground,
While the crowd looked on in horror and no one dared make
    a sound,
Every one in the tent was spellbound as he raised him over
    his head,
And then with an effort, hurled him to the ground; the
    Captain was dead.

And then the victorious Cuban said, his voice loud enough
    to be heard
By all who had witnessed the struggle, "Now! who dares
    say I'm a cur?
'Tis you who are curs; you're all cowards; you're killing our
    children and wives
But when you meet our men in battle you tremble and run
    for your lives.

" You've stolen our money in taxes; you've burned all our
    houses and barns,
Killed off all our fowl and cattle; destroyed all our factories
    and farms.

We men are fighting for freedom; liberty henceforth is our
    queen,
But you who have never known bondage know not what
    liberty means.

" The men in our ranks will die fighting; this country you'll
    never regain!
I'd rather by far spy for Cuba than command all the armies
    of Spain.
That's all. I admit I am guilty; my duty has made me a
    spy.
Don't hang me! I fought like a soldier; like a soldier let
    me die."

As he said this his voice became husky, his strength seemed
    almost gone
A voice rang out through the silence, " To hang such a man
    would be wrong! "
Another voice called for the sentence; as he rose the judge
    heaved a sigh,
" My duty has made me your judge and I command you be
    shot as a spy."

They placed him under guard until sunrise, then led him
    out to die.
Two men were sent to blindfold him but he pushed them
    both aside.
" I'll not be blindfolded; keep your bandage for cowards,"
    he said,
" I want to watch for its coming; to me 'tis a glorious
    death! "

Then came the command and they fired; he fell with a smile
    on his face.
He knew that he died as a soldier without any mark of
    disgrace;

His enemies gathered around him for soldiers admire the
  brave,
And they tenderly buried his body and marked his a soldiers
  grave.

JAMES W. STANISTREET

❖ ❖ ❖

MAMMY'S TREASUH

Mammy's treasuh settin' theah
    Snug up side de doh
What you lookin' at, ma chile —
    What you waitin' foh?

Seein' things an' hearin' things
    Mammy knows ain't thauh —
She done tole you so befoh;
    You don' peah to cauh.

Once you says you hea'd a voice
    Low down neah de grass
Says you shadder talked to you
    When you tried to pass.

Mammy were so skeered she run
    You come runnin' close
Ketched yoh Mammy by de han'
    Made her upset mos'.

Chile, you dreams away de day
    Settin' heah by me,
Findin' pictures in de sky
    What you gwine to be?

Tell me, Lord, what's in ma trust
    Show me what to do —
Some ob dis yere chile am mine
    But most belongs to You!

ALICE DRAKE

❖   ❖   ❖

FREE LITTLE CHILLUNS ON DE FLO'

Free pickaninnies on de flo'
    Look mighty cute an' wise.
Dey all am lookin' out de do'
    Wif bright an' shinin' eyes.

De brown one hab an open mouf
    Two folded little hands.
One wears a hat upon his haid
    Wid outen any bands.

When dese po' niggas go to he'ben
    Up whar de angels stand,
I wonda will dey all be white
    Jus' like de angel band.

Will all dese chilluns be alike
    Bof white an brack de same?
Or will de good ones jus' be white
    An' bad ones brack remain?

Dars many white ones should be brack
    An' many brack ones white.
De good Lawd knows how it should be
    An' he will make it right.

JOHN MC MASTER

AN IRISH THING IN RHYME

Under Kitty's Window

" Ah thin, who is that there talkin' ? "
   " Sure it's only me, ye know —
I was thinkin' we'd go walkin' — "
   " Were ye raly thinkin' so? "

" Ah ye needn't be so cruel
   An me thrudged this sivin mile! "
" It is cruel, Michael jewel?
   Sure I'm dressin' all the while! "

Before Michael's Cottage

" There now, that's me cottage Kitty! "
   " Is it Mike? "
" Yis, and isn't it pretty? "
   " Hm — lonesome like. "

" Lonesome! " (now's yer minute
   Michael strike)
" Sure, if you wor in it — "
   " Arrah, Mike! "

ELSA KEELING

SHAUN O'NEILL

One evenin' as I walked through thon leafy glen
   I met Shaun O'Neill lonely wanderin',
Says I, " Ye've the grand aisy times, ye young men,
   On what is it that ye are ponderin' ? "
     Says I,
" On what is it ye are ponderin' ? "

His big blue eyes sought mine, an' then sought the ground,
    An' stutterin' an' stammerin' an' blinkin',
Says he, " I've been here, this last hour, walkin' round,
    An' 'twas on your sweet self I was thinkin',"
        Says he,
" 'Twas on your sweet self I was thinkin'."

Says I, " Ye ha' no right to think about me,"
    Though my heart it was jumpin' an' leapin'.
Says he, " I can't help it — I'm thinkin' o' ye
    Night an' day, whether wakin' or sleepin'."
        Says he,
" Oh I dream o' ye wakin' an' sleepin'! "

" I've been watchin' to see ye come down through the glen
    To tell you fer your love I'm dyin' — "
Says I, " Och, there's nothin' I hate like the men " —
    (May the Lord forgive me fer lyin' !)
        Says I,
(May the Lord forgive me fer lyin' !)

Says he, " Well at that rate, do no more I can
    Though me heart'll be broken wi' sorra."
Say I, " I hate men, but yet love one man —
    An' maybe I'll meet him the morra."
        I called,
" Shaun dear! will ye meet me the morra? "

                                    PADRIC GREGORY

❖   ❖   ❖

THE DRIP OF THE IRISH RAIN

    Nature has surely the gift of tongues,
        In my own land far away;
    An' one among 'em I'm missin' sore,
        An' more wid each passin' day;

Not lilt of the bee, nor lay of the breeze,
    Nor thrill o' the blackbird's sthrain —
I'm lovin' 'em all, but it's lonesome most,
    For the dhrip of the Irish rain!

Now fallin' soft from the hoverin' clouds
    Like the croon of a lullaby,
For the homesick flowers that wor once as stars
    Set high in the archin' sky;
Now wid thud in the thatch, an' tap at the hatch,
    An' tinkle agin the pane
Givin' us greetin' an' cheer betimes —
    The sootherin' Irish rain!

An' whin it has passed how the earth laughs out,
    In the face o' the cl'arin' sky!
"Is it rainin' it was?" says the laggard sun —
    "Ah thin let me kiss you dhry."
The soople daisies listen an' lift,
    An' the dog-rose br'athes again,
An' cowslips whisper to fairy-flax
    The praise of the tindher rain!

From a cuddled thrush in the hedges hush
    A clear "come-all-ye" rings,
An' all the blessed stillness stirs
    Wid the whirr of unfoldin' wings,
Till you think of a Dhruid among his choir,
    Whin the wood was the warrior's fane,
An' great oaks 'fended the Beltaine firs
    From the dhrip of the passin' rain!

There's a spot near the heart of the ould land set
    An' the best of my life is there,
Where dust wid dust has for centuries met
    To the measure of keen an' prayer;

'Tis long since the chrism of lovin' tears
　　On its shroudin' green has lain.
But to freshen it still, at God's dear will
　　Comes the dhrip of the Irish rain!

No wonder its message lingers thin;
　　For oh, like the Banshees moan,
It's only for ear of the Celt to hear
　　The message within its tone;
An' loyal hearts of the exiles know
　　That for raquaim and refrain
They would choose some day (an' 'twor theirs to say)
　　The dhrip of the Irish rain!

MARGARET M. HALVEY

❖　❖　❖

THE TAKING OF 'TONIO

'Tonio Baldi ees fast lika snail,
Wanta mak' love but he don'ta know how;
Try to gat marry, but alla time fail —
Rosa Baratta she's feex eet all now!

Three, four, fi' time deesa 'Tonio try
Catches some girl he would like for hees wife:
Like seeck cow he would grunta an' sigh,
Talkin' about how so lonely hees life.
Sometheeng like dat he would tal dem to show
Mebbe some day he ees gona say more.
But dat's so far as he evve would go —
So, ees no wondra da girls gotta sore.

'Tonio call on da Rosa wan night,
An' da first meenute, so soon as he came,
'Tonio say: " Mees Baratt', eef I might,
I would like calla you by your first name " —

[179]

Dat ees da time dat she land da poor feesh!
Queeck she say: " 'Tonio, s'posa you do.
Call me my firsta name — an' eef you weesh,
Call me by your owna lasta name, too."

'Tonio Baldi was fast lika snail,
Wanta gat marry, but deedn't know how:
Here ees wan time dat he joust could no fail —
Rosa B. Baldi ees feex eet all now!

✿   ✿   ✿   ✿   ✿   ✿   ✿   ✿   ✿   ✿

PROSE FOR
READING AND RECITATION

A CHRISTMAS PRESENT FOR A LADY

It was the week before Christmas and the First Reader class had almost to a man, decided on the gifts to be lavished on " Teacher." But Morris Mogilewsky, whose love for teacher was far greater than the combined loves of all the other children, had as yet, no present to bestow. The knowledge saddened all his hours and was the more maddening because it could in no wise be shared by teacher. She had noticed his altered bearing and tried with all sorts of artful beguilements to make him happy and at ease. But her efforts served only to increase his unhappiness and his love. And he loved her — oh how he loved her! And now when the other boys and girls were preparing surprises and gifts of price for teacher, his hands were as empty as his heart was full. Appeal to his mother met with denial, prompt and energetic.

" For what you go and make over Christmas brasunts? You ain't no Krisht; you should better have no kindt feelings over Krishts, neither. Your Papa could to have a madt."

" All the other fellows buys her brasunts, undt I'm loving mit her too. It's polite I gives her brasunts the while I'm got such a kindt feeling over her! "

" Well, we ain't got no money for buy nothings and your Papa has all times a scare he shouldn't get no more." So Morris was helpless and teacher all unknowing.

And the great day, the Friday before Christmas came. The school was for the first half-hour, quite mad. Room 18 generally so placid and peaceful was a howling wilderness full of brightly colored groups of children all whispering, all giggling, and hiding queer bundles.

Isadore Bolchatosky was the first to lay tribute before teacher. He came forward with a sweet smile and a tall candlestick, and teacher, for a moment could not be made

[183]

to understand that all the length of bluish white china was really hers " for keeps."

" It's tomorrow holiday," Isadore assured her, " and ve gifs you brasunts the while we have a kindt feeling. Candlesticks could to cost twenty-five cents."

" Oh, it's a lie; three for ten! " said a voice in the background but teacher hastened to respond to Isadore's test of her credulity.

" Indeed they could. This candlestick could have cost fifty cents and it's just what I want. It is very good of you to bring me a present."

" You're welcome, alright," said Isadore retiring. And then, the ice being broken, the First Reader class, in a body, rose to cast its gifts on teacher's desk and its arms around teacher's neck.

Nathan Horrowitz presented a small cup and saucer. Isadore Applebaum bestowed a large calendar for the year before last; Sadie Gonorowsky brought a basket containing a bottle of perfume, a thimble and a bright silk handkerchief; Sara Schrowsky offered a pen wiper and a celluloid collar button, and Eva Kedansky gave an elaborate nasal douche under the pleasing delusion that it was an atomizer. Jacob Spitsky pressed forward with a tortoise shell comb of terrifying aspect and hungry teeth, and an air showing forth a determination to adjust it in its destined place. Teacher meekly bowed her head and Jacob forced his offering into her long-suffering hair and departed with the information, " Cost fifteen cents, Teacher."

Meanwhile the rush of presentation went steadily on. Bottles of perfume vied with one another and with the all-pervading soap until the air was heavy and breathing grew laborious. But pride swelled the hearts of the assembled multitude. No other teacher had so many presents. No other was so beloved.

When the waste paper basket had been twice filled with

wrappings and twice emptied; when order was emerging out of chaos; when the Christmas tree had been disclosed and its treasures distributed, a timid little hand was laid on teacher's knee and a plaintive voice whispered, " Say, Teacher, I got something for you," and teacher turned quickly to see Morris, her dearest boy charge.

" Now, Morris, you shouldn't have troubled to get me a present; you know you and I are such good friends that — "

" Teacher, yiss mam," Morris interrupted in a bewitching and rising inflection of his soft and plaintive voice. " I know you got a kindt feeling by me and I couldn't to tell even how I got a kindt feeling by you. Only it's about that kindt feeling I should give you a brasunt. I didn't to have no soap nor no perfumery and my Mama she couldn't to buy none by the store; but Teacher, I've got something awful nice for you by brasunt."

" And what is it, dear? What is my new present? "

" Teacher, it's like this, I don't know; I ain't so big like I could know. It ain't for boys; it's for ladies. Over yesterday on the night comes my Papa to my house and he gives my Mama the brasunt. Sooner she looks on it, soon she has a glad, an awful glad. In her eyes stands tears, and she says, like that, out of Jewish, " Thanks," and she keeses my Papa a kees. Und my Papa, how he is polite! he says, like that, out of Jewish too, " You're welcome all right," und he keeses my Mama a kees. So my Mama she sets and look on the brasunt, and all the time she looks she has a glad over it. Und I didn't to have no soap, so you could to have the brasunt."

" But, Morris, did your mother say I might? "

" Teacher, no mam, she didn't to say like that and she didn't to say not like that; she didn't to know. But it's for ladies, und I didn't to have no soap. You could to look on it. It ain't for boys."

And here Morris opened a hot little hand and disclosed a tightly folded pinkish paper. As teacher read it he watched her with eager furtive eyes, dry and bright, until her eyes grew suddenly moist and his promptly followed suit. As she looked down at him he made his moan once more, " It's for ladies und I didn't to have no soap."

" But Morris dear," cried teacher unsteadily, laughing a little and yet not far from tears, " this is ever so much nicer than soap and you're quite right it is for ladies and I never had one in all my life before."

" You're welcome, all right. That's how my Papa says, it is polite. Und my Mama she keeses my Papa a kees."

" Well? "

" Well, you ain't never keesed me a kees, und I seen how you keesed Eva Gonorowsky. I'm loving mit you too. Why don't you never kees me a kees? "

" Perhaps," suggested teacher mischievously, " perhaps it ain't for boys."

" Teacher, yis mam, it's for boys," he cried as he felt her arms around him and saw that in her eyes too " stands tears."

Late that night teacher sat in her pretty room and reviewed her treasures. She saw that they were very numerous, very touching, very whimsical, and very precious. But above all the rest she cherished a frayed and pinkish paper, rather crumpled, and a little soiled. For it held the love of a man and a woman, and a little child, and the magic of a home, for Morris Mogilewsky's Christmas present for ladies was the receipt for a month's rent for a room on the top floor of a Monroe Street tenement.

MYRA KELLEY

"RUNNIN' ERRANDS"

Aw gee, ma, do I have to go to the store now? You make me go every single afternoon. Why can't *Dot* go get the groceries, huh? — Aw, what if she *is* a "little lady," it won't hurt her to carry home a few pounds of sugar, will it? — All right, then, I'll go in a few minutes. You don't have to make me go to the store the minute I get home from school, do you? Well, then, I'll go pretty soon, but I want to rest a few minutes first.

(Sinks into a chair) Gee, ma, I feel awful queer today! — Oh, I don't know just what's the matter with me, but I feel sorta sick. I don't have to go to the store and lugg home all the groceries when I'm sick, do I? — Aw, you don't care how bad I feel. You're just as mean to me as you can be! Say, ma, it's raining out! M-hm! It started to rain when I was coming home from school. If I go to the store when it's raining, I'm liable to get my feet wet and catch cold and die. Then who'd go to the store for you? — But maybe I'd just as soon die, anyhow! Then I wouldn't have to be runnin' errands all the time. I'll bet Saint Peter wouldn't send me on any errands. They don't have grocery stores in heaven — or *any* kind of stores!

Say, ma, can I go ever to Joe Fogarty's first, and do my homework over at his house? — Aw, but I *wouldn't* get wet just going over *there!* He only lives across the street. — Well, ma, if I go to the store for you, will you give me a nickel so's I can get an ice cream cone? — Aw, you never give me anything. You're just as mean to me as you can be! — Can I have a piece of cake before I go? — There is *too* some left! There was a piece left this morning when I went to school. Who ate it, I'd like to know? — Aw, you make me sick, taking the last piece of cake!

Well, I'm going in the other room and play the victrola. I can't help it if you *are* in a hurry. I'm not going to the store now. — I'm tired! — What? If I go now, you'll take me to the — *circus* — tomorrow? Aw gee, ma, that's great! You're just as good to me as you can be! What do you want me to get for you, huh?

ELEANOR F. KING

❖ ❖ ❖

THE STORY KATHIE TOLD

Now, stay right still and listen, kitty-cat, and I'll tell you a story.

Once there was a little girl.

She was a pretty good little girl, and minded her papa 'n' mamma everything they said, only sometimes she didn't, and then she was naughty; but she was always sorry, and said she wouldn't do so any more, and her mamma'd forgive her.

So she was going to hang up her stocking.

"You'll have to be pretty good, 'less 'twon't be filled," said her mamma.

"'Less maybe there'll be a big bunch of sticks in it," said her papa.

Do you think that's a nice way to talk, kitty-cat? I don't.

So the little girl was good as she could be, 'less she was bigger, and didn't cry and slap her little sister hardly any at tall, and always minded her mamma when she came where the chimney was, 'specially much.

So she hung up her stocking.

And in the night she got awake, and wanted it to come morning; but in the morning she didn't get awake till 'twas all sunshiny out doors.

Then she ran quick as she could to look at her stocking where she'd hung it; and true's you live, kitty-cat, there wasn't the leastest thing in it — not the leastest little mite of a scrimp!

Oh, the little girl felt dreadfully! How'd you feel, s'pose it had been you, kitty-cat?

She 'menced to cry, the little girl did, and she kept going harder 'n' harder, till by 'mby she screeched orfly, and her mamma came rushing to see what the matter was.

"Mercy me!" said her mamma. "Look over by the window 'fore you do that any more, Kathie."

That little girl's name was Kathie too, kitty-cat, just the same's mine.

So she looked over by the window, the way her mamma said, and — oh! there was the loveliest dolly's house you ever saw in all your born life.

It had curtains to pull to the sides when you wanted to play, and pull in front when you didn't.

There was a bedroom, kitty-cat, and a diner-room, and a kitchen, and a parlor, and they all had carpets on.

And there was the sweetest dolly in the parlor, all dressed up in blue silk! Oh, dear! And a penano, to play real little tunes on, and a rocking-chair, and — O kitty-cat! I can't begin to tell you half 'bout it.

I can't about the bedroom, either, nor the diner-room.

But the kitchen was the very bestest of all. There was a stove — a teenty tonty mite of a one, kitty-cat, — with dishes just 'zactly like mamma's, only littler, of course, and fry-pans and everything; and spoons to stir with, and a rolling-pin, and the two little cutters-out, and the darlingest baker-sheet ever you saw!

And the first thing that little girl did was to make some teenty mites of cookies, 'cause her mamma let her; and if you'll come right down stairs, kitty-cat, I'll give you one.

'Cause I was that little girl, kitty-cat, all the time.

❖ ❖ ❖

JOHN BROWN'S SISTER'S WEDDING

Sue ought to have been married a long while ago. That's what everybody says who knows her. She has been engaged to Mr. Travers for three years, and has had to refuse lots of offers to go to the circus with other young men. I have wanted her to get married, so that I could go and live with her and Mr. Travers. When I think that if it hadn't been for a mistake I made she would have been married yesterday, I find it dreadfully hard to be resigned. But we ought always to be resigned to everything when we can't help it.

Before I go any further I must tell about my printing-press. It belonged to Tom McGinnis, but he got tired of it and sold it to me real cheap. He was going to exchange it for a bicycle, a St. Bernard dog, and twelve good books, but he finally let me have it for a dollar and a half.

It prints beautifully, and I have printed cards for ever so many people, and made three dollars and seventy cents already. I thought it would be nice to be able to print circus bills in case Tom and I should ever have another circus, so I sent to the city and bought some type more than an inch high, and some beautiful yellow paper.

Last week it was finally agreed that Sue and Mr. Travers should be married without waiting any longer. You should have seen what a state of mind she and mother were in. They did nothing but buy new clothes, and sew, and talk about the wedding all day long. Sue was determined to be married in church, and to have six bridesmaids and six bridegrooms, and flowers and music and all sorts of things. The only thing that troubled her was making up her mind who to invite. Mother wanted her to invite Mr. and Mrs. McFadden and the seven McFadden girls, but Sue said they had insulted her, and she couldn't bear the idea of asking the McFadden tribe. Everbody agreed that old Mr. Wilkinson, who once came to a party at our house with one boot and one slipper, couldn't be invited; but it was decided that every one else that was on good terms with our family should have an invitation.

Sue counted up all the people she meant to invite, and there was nearly three hundred of them. You would hardly believe it, but she told me that I must carry around all the invitations and deliver them myself. Of course I couldn't do this without neglecting my studies and losing time, which is always precious, so I thought of a plan which would save Sue the trouble of directing three hundred invitations and save me from wasting time in delivering them.

I got to work with my printing-press, and printed a dozen splendid big bills about the wedding. When they were printed I cut a lot of small pictures of animals and ladies riding on horses out of some old circus bills and pasted them on the wedding bills. They were perfectly gorgeous, and you could see them four or five rods off. When they were all done I made some paste in a tin pail, and went out after dark and pasted them in good places all over the village.

The next afternoon father came into the house looking very stern, and carrying one of the wedding bills in his hand. He handed it to Sue and said: " Susan, what does this mean? These bills are posted all over the village, and there are crowds of people reading them." Sue read the bill, and then she gave an awful shriek, and fainted away, and I hurried down to the post-office to see if the mail had

NOSES

A Boy's Composition

Everybody's got a nose, but they ain't all alike, 'cept a fish wat aint got no nose 'cause they don't smell till they git old — then they do smell orful. Birds and ducks and ostriches and chickens and turkeys has got noses, but they don't show them cause they is most all on the insides out of the way and they has to catch bugs and things so quick that they don't get to smell 'em till they is inside their mouths. Girls and elephants and anteaters has got noses but they is all different. My girl has got the nicest nose what I ever seen and she noses it. A elephant's got a orful funny nose too what he uses for a water pot to sprinkle fellers with when they fool him and wot makes him look like he's got a tail on both ends. A anteater has got a funny nose too, but I don't believe a anteater would eat my ant 'cause she is so cross and old. Sometimes a nose is awful bother specially when you are a-eatin' limburger cheese. When you gits old your nose and your chin gits very intermate, and when the nose gits tired it jist goes and rests on the chin, which is very kind 'cause the chin don't git tired, specially female chins but jist chins and chins till time is old and gray. It's the funniest thing that some men's noses is as red as fire; ma says that is because they look upon the wine when it is red — they is also called nosegays. Noses is used to blow with and snore with, which is very useful in churches and sleepin' cars. A dog's nose is cold but he makes it warm for burglars and cats and things. Trees and flowers blows in the spring and summer, but the nose blows all the year round.

HENRY FIRTH WOOD

BORROWING A STAMP FROM SISTER

The scene is a bedroom. Marion, the elder sister is seated at a desk writing busily. Great piles of material are on the desk denoting the fact that big sister has an endless job before her. Jane, the younger sister enters and speaks softly.

Jane: Marion, would you mind if —

Marion: Don't disturb me now please: can't you see that I'm busy? If you want something go get it!

Jane (very meekly): Excuse me, I didn't realize you were still writing. I thought you would have stopped after two hours and a half. (She tiptoes across the room to the desk and tries to open one of the desk drawers without attracting too much attention, but this is impossible because Marion's work is all over the desk.)

Marion (irritably): What are you looking for?

Jane (softly): A stamp.

Marion: Why are you looking for a stamp?

Jane (with a flash of fire): You told me if I wanted something to go get it.

Marion: Well, I didn't mean it! Why do you want a stamp?

Jane: So that I can mail these three letters.

Marion: Oh, I see. You want three stamps. Where are your own, please?

Jane: I'm afraid I haven't got any.

Marion: You never have any.

Jane: Oh, Marion, how can you say that?

Marion: Because it's perfectly true, and you know it is. You've never been known to have a stamp in your life. This is the third time this week you've come in here to borrow stamps, and I'm just sick of it.

Jane: Oh, but Marion —

Marion (with withering sarcasm): Yes, I know, always the same thing. The poor little darling must have a stamp. Honestly, I've never seen such a girl! You never have anything of your own. Always borrowing something from me. I'm always lending you things or giving you things, for that's what it amounts to, and yet you never have anything of your own. You never have a complete set of anything. Last year you didn't have any nightgowns, and I had to give you some. The year before that it was something else.

Jane: Oh, Marion!

Marion: Well it's true, every word of it! You either never take the trouble to buy what you need or else you just up and lose all your things. I don't know what you do with your belongings! (With a sudden change in her voice) Are those letters important?

Jane: I never write unimportant letters.

Marion: Where are they going?

Jane (defiantly): I guess those letters are my business.

Marion: Oh are they? Well then you can find your stamps somewhere else. (A voice from the distance, exceedingly high pitched and faint) Girls what are you arguing about?

Marion: It's the same old thing Mother — the poor little thing wants a stamp!

Mother: Well, can't you lend her one, dear?

Marion (her voice raised): One! She wants three! And I'm sick of handing everything I have out to her and I'm sick of seeing her have her own way in everything! A little discipline would do her a world of good, if you want my opinion on the subject!

Mother: I'm sorry dear, but I can't hear a word you're saying, but won't you please stop arguing?

Marion: There now, see what you've done? You've been keeping Mother awake!

Jane: Not at all. You were doing the talking. All I've done is to ask you to lend me —

Marion: Go on and take the old stamps. That's what you're aiming at and you know you always get them in the end. I always have to give them to you, and all this talk about lending them to you is bunk, because you know you've never paid me back for one in your life. But go on and take them and leave me in peace. Just before you go however, there is one thing that I would like to say to you and that is, please don't leave this house today without either sending William for a complete set of stamps or else going to the postoffice yourself and buying them!

Jane: Thank you so awfully much.

Marion: Don't bother to thank me, and please understand that this is absolutely the last time that I am going to lend you anything. From now on you will please use your own possessions.

(Jane is about to retire from the field not bloody but bowed when Mother appears in the doorway, goes to Marion's clothes closet and rummages among the contents. Jane looks on with interest. Finally Mother triumphantly produces a very handsome wrap).

[196]

Mother: Marion, I wish you would learn to return my clothes to my closet.

(Jane giggles, Marion glares, and Jane dances out waving the stamps).

Jane: I'm glad she can't wear mine!

POLLY KING

❖ ❖ ❖

THE MYSTERY OF THE DOLL'S HOUSE

Her house being all settled and in order Mariette has invited her best friends for tea. Mariette is a lovely doll and she has donned for the occasion a pink silk tea gown; she wears her pretty pink bead necklace and she is seated in a big arm chair before the table on which stands a large silver tea-urn and piles of cakes and sweets. The guests, the dolls I mean, Fanfan, Lucy, Patonilla, Clè-Clè and Josephine are very flattered because they are the first guests in Mariette's charming house. It is like one of those handsome buildings one sees in the Champs-Elysées. On the ground floor is the drawing room for receiving, hung with pale blue silk; the furniture is covered with brocade to match, which suits the complexions of the ladies admirably. Little fatty Patonilla is seated at the piano and keeps playing " Au clair de la lune." On the first floor there is a sea-green bedroom with a bed and silken coverlid, next to the bedroom, a bath-room and dressing room show the modern appliances of comfort in perfection. On the second floor, the study lined with books and the governess, Mamz'elle, is standing in dignified attitude with her eye-glass perched on her nose, before the black-board on which is written Ba — ba —

At six o'clock the windows, with their pink curtains drawn in the middle by a ribbon just like a sash, the mysterious windows are lighted up. Mariette leaves her chair and begs to be excused for a moment to give some sugar to the horses that are stabled behind the little house. The guests who are just a little jealous and love to find fault, lose no time in saying nasty things about their hostess.

"The cakes were very dry," declares Fanfan.

"The coffee cream tastes of vanilla," says Lucy.

"The piano is out of tune," cries Patonilla.

"When is the chocolate coming," groans Clè-Clè.

But Josephine says, "You have not noticed the funniest of all. The house . . . " she hesitates and all the little heads draw nearer to listen. Then in a whisper but with triumph in her voice Josephine tells the great secret. "The house has no staircase!"

HENRI DUVERNOIS

❖ ❖ ❖

CHRISTOPHER COBB

Had Christopher Cobb, on a certain June morning, been looking for a character instead of angle worms, he need have gone no further than the apple tree back of the school house. It was the eleven o'clock recess and certain beginghamed ones of authority were discussing the principal topic of the day, Christopher Cobb.

"He's got the puggedist nose and the most freckles of any boy in school."

"He's the worst speller."

"He's mean and cruel, and that's what he is! He sat on my pet cat the day I brought it to school and he never said he was sorry."

The bell rang and the enthusiastic young teacher had a plan that far outreached any former history of Wilson Corners.

"Now, children, I propose that we close school this year — with — a picnic at Waterford Glen."

[198]

Every one of the sixteen faces beamed with satisfaction.

"And, now, children, I am going to ask each boy to invite a girl to go with him to the picnic, and moreover, he must hold himself responsible for the safe arrival of both girl and lunch basket at the grounds. And — that the girls may enjoy themselves the more, each boy is expected to bring a fishing pole for the girl."

A frown of stolid gloom settled on each boy's face. Once outside they gathered in a corner of the playground and boiled over.

"Ask a girl to go to a picnic — well I guess not!" was the general decision.

Under the apple tree the girls buzzed. Their problem was — which boy would ask them. There was an even number in the school. Then someone thought of Christopher Cobb. Who'd want to go with him?

"Oh Sally, I bet he'll ask you, because one day I saw him show you his pet collection of marbles," said Mary Ellen. Patience Winthrop added that she'd seen Christopher give Sally a bird's nest and these were considered unfailing signs of Christopher's choice. Sally blushed but no one envied her.

Three days passed and not a girl had been asked to go to the picnic. On the fourth day Mathew, the courageous, marched up to Sally with a brave face but a beating heart. "Say, Sally, will — will you go with me to the picnic?"

"Oh, Mathew, I'm sorry but I-I-I can't."

"Why can't you?"

"I'm going with someone else."

A gasp of surprise came from the beginghamed group.

"Oh Sally, when did he ask you?"

"Why didn't you tell us?"

"I couldn't. It's a secret."

And hereupon the beginghamed group decided to make their partnerships secret too.

On the day before the picnic Christopher was accosted with, " Say Chris, who you going to take to the picnic? "

" Ain't going to take no girl! "

" Teacher said you had to take somebody."

" Well I ain't takin' any girl."

That afternoon Sally dragged dusty feet toward home and the sorest heart that ever beat under a gingham apron.

" Oh, how will I ever live through tomorrow? All Wilson Corners will know I told a lie." Then Sally stopped. Just there the road ran by the brook, and back of a clump of bushes a boy was tying a string to a fishing pole. Sally's heart stopped for one whole beat. The boy looked up and Sally, gulping, said, " Hello."

" Hello, what are you doing here? "

" I came to fish," said Sally, hardly believing her own boldness.

" Hump, where's your pole? "

" I thought you'd let me use yours."

Christopher considered for a moment. " Well, you can't have my best one but this one will be all right for you. Girls can't fish anyhow."

They fished a long time in silence. Then Sally whispered, " Going to the picnic tomorrow, Chris? "

" Nope."

" Why ain't you goin'? "

" O 'cause I don't want to. You're going ain't you? "

" I — I guess so."

" Who you going with? "

Sally felt that she was taking a long chance but she said, " I'm going with you."

Christopher may have been taken aback but he ignored Sally's statement. Then all of a sudden, " Gee, I got a bite — get out of the way! "

When he'd brought the fish out he declared it to be the best he'd ever done and Sally rejoiced with him. Then they resumed their silence. Sally sent up a little prayer, "Dear God, please let me catch a fish as big as Christopher's." Her prayer must have been heard because in a little while Sally felt a tug.

"Oh Chris, I got a bite — ooh — there he is!"

"Gimme that line. You can't land him. He's too big for you."

"Christopher Cobb, you stay just where you are. I'm going to land this myself!"

There was a Spartan light in Sally's eye but the strain was too much for her tender muscles — she slipped in the soft soil and when Christopher reached her she stood wet and dripping at the bottom.

"Where's the fish?"

"He got away. The line cut my hand," Sally was almost weeping, not from the physical hardship but from chagrin.

"Lemme see, gee! It must hurt like fun, don't it?" In some mysterious way Chris's heart was softened.

"If only that fish hadn't got away! But he was a big one, wasn't he, Chris?"

"Well you was plucky anyhow, dead plucky!"

"Well, I guess I'd better go home," said Sally.

"Guess you had," said Chris. "And say, Sally — "

"Yes, Chris?"

"It's all right about the picnic tomorrow. I'll be round nine sharp."

Christopher had had a change of heart but whether it was because of Sally's spunk or her helplessness nobody knows.

❖   ❖   ❖

TOMMY, THE UNTAINTED

"Shut up! Shut up!" whispered Tommy to himself. Yes, it had a truly beautiful sound, but a bit daring if the injunction were addressed to the wrong person. Ah! but Tommy would manage that; never fear! With inward delight he murmured the words. Yes, they were just the words to quell his too unrespectful sister and his far too presuming friend.

He rose, rolled the rich words around his tongue, and then started in search of his sister. She was sitting tranquilly on the seat of the swing.

" Gimme a swing," ordered Tommy.

" Say, I got here first," claimed his sister.

" Well, then, it's my turn," stated Tommy grandly.

" Oh, it is, is it? " Of course ladies don't sneer but at that moment Lois came perilously near losing all claims to ladyship.

" Yes, an' if you don't give it to me, I'll — I'll pull the seat from unner you, an' then where'll you be, huh? " As it was quite obvious where Lois would be, she disdained to reply.

" And," pursued Tommy, " if you're not off by the time I count ten, I'll climb up the tree and joggle you."

For one moment Lois' sweet blue eyes flashed; then with cruel brevity she said, " Shut up! "

Tommy could hardly believe his ears. His words, his magic words that he had scarcely dared say aloud as yet, had been blatantly addressed to him, to Tommy Cotter. With true instinct of the artist, he had been saving this gem until the appropriate time, but now he could never say the words to Lois. For a wild moment he thought of saying, " Shut up yourself! " But Lois would be just conceited enough to think he was imitating her. He moved away, sorely wounded and bitterly reflecting that he had never cared much for Lois anyhow. But as he turned the corner of the house he had an inspiration. Virtuously he called back, " Lois Cotter, I'm s'prised at you, and I've a good mind to tell Mama on you." But Lois was swinging hard and carolling lustily, " I want to be a sun-beam."

" A sunbeam! " sniffed Tommy. With a feeling of dis-illusionment, he scuffed his way towards the open garage door. Sitting in the doorway was Tommy's younger sister Sue.

" Oh, Tummy, see my p'itty 'ittle Kitty? Tummy, I named her after you, only I call her Tummylette."

Tommy snorted and rolled his morsel with exquisite relish. " Shut up." He was not prepared for the effect on Sue. She rolled up into a round pink ball and gurgled helplessly. Finally she suppressed her giggles and lisped, " Thay it again, Tummy; thay it again! " But Tommy was not so cheap as all that, so Sue said it for him. " Thet ep! Thet ep! "

Across the lawn came the mother of Lois and Tommy and Sue.

" Thet ep, Mama! Oh, thet ep! " screamed Sue joyfully, fearful lest Tommy should say the words first. But Tommy had retreated. He reached the back street intending to look up a friend, when Willy Kemper strolled up.

" Lo, Tom."

" Hi, Bill."

" C'mon over to my house. See the penny I found."

" Where'd you find it? "

" Unner your back gate."

" Hand it over then; it b'longs to me, Willy Kemper! "

" It does not! You wouldn't never have thought of it if I hadn't told you I'd found it." All this time they had been progressing towards Tommy's house and stood by the now deserted swing.

" Oh shut up! " ordered Tommy, realizing anew the de-licious tang of it. Eyes and mouth opened and Willy gazed and gazed at Tommy; then with a deep, throaty chuckle he doubled up on the swing, always a perilous thing to do. But there is a special god who carefully guards the lives of all people of avoirdupois, and Willy remained on the swing.

"All fat people take it the same way," said Tommy complacently as if "it" had been the measles.

"Where'd you get it?" inquired Willy.

"Oh, I jus' happened to think of it. It just come in my head," said Tommy.

A light appeared in Willy's eyes; it was the light of dawning shrewdness, and with deplorable tactlessness he addressed Tommy thus: "I bet you the penny I found, that you didn't think of it yourself."

Thus reminded of their former spat Tommy was especially angry when he said, "I did so! "

"You didn't! "

"Did so! "

"Didn't! " Much more of such repartee and then coursing across the lawn were two figures — the one in the rear was fat and breathless but still game for it managed to gasp, "Shut up! Shut up! "

Lois watching the scene from the kitchen door called shrewishly, "Give it to him Will." Thus spurred on, Willy gained in speed. It was too much for Lois to remain passive and she joined in the chase yelling with much vigor, "Shut up Tommy Cotter, shut up! " Sue not to be outdone, dropped her Tummylette and trundled along in the rear, piping out, "Thet ep, thet ep! "

That night, Tommy having been relegated to bed at the usual humiliating hour heard his parents conversing in the room below. Mrs. Cotter was speaking. "Yes, Tommy was the only one who behaved decently, and Robert I don't think we ought to let Tommy go with that little Willy Kemper. I know that neither Lois nor Sue would ever have thought of saying such a thing if it hadn't been for Willy. And Robert, I can tell you, I felt real proud of Tommy when he didn't say 'shut up' back to them."

[204]

Mr. Cotter laughed tolerantly. "Oh, I guess our Tommy's a pretty good kid."

And Tommy was asleep by then.

BETTY COLLINS

❖ ❖ ❖

THE NATIONAL FLAG

There is the national flag. He must be cold indeed, who can look upon its folds rippling in the breeze without pride of country. Who, as he sees it, can think of a state merely? Whose eyes, once fastened upon its radiant trophies, can fail to recognize the image of the whole nation? It has been called a "floating piece of poetry," and yet I know not if it have an intrinsic beauty beyond other ensigns. Its highest beauty is in that which it symbolizes. It is because of what it represents that all gaze at it with delight and reverence. It is a piece of bunting lifted in the air, but it speaks sublimely, and every part has a voice. Its stripes of alternate red and white proclaim the original union of thirteen states to maintain the Declaration of Independence. Its stars of white on a field of blue proclaim that union of states constituting our national constellation, which received a new star with every new state. The two together signify union, past and present. The very colors have a language which was officially recognized by our fathers. White is for purity, red for valor, blue for justice; and all together, bunting, stripes, stars and colors blazing in the sky, make the flag of our country to be cherished by all our hearts, to be upheld by all our hands.

CHARLES SUMNER

WARNING

George had been warned that the green apples that were growing in his grandmother's yard would be bad for his stomach, but one day the temptation became too great and he was seen with one of the big, green beauties meditating deeply, then was heard to exclaim:

"On your mark! Get ready! Lookout, stomach, it's a-coming!"

❖ ❖ ❖

THE CHOCOLATY LANGUAGE

An English professor had been trying very hard to correct the many errors in speech made by his five-year-old daughter. The other day he took her to call on her aunt and at tea Murial was given a large piece of cake.

"Oh, I just love chocolate cake!" she exclaimed. "It's awfully nice."

"Murial dear," corrected Daddy, "it is wrong to say that you ' love ' cake, and I've frequently pointed out that ' just ' is unnecessary in such a sentence. Again, ' awfully ' is quite wrong: ' very ' would be correct. Now repeat your remark, please."

Murial obediently repeated: "I like chocolate cake; it is very good."

There was a pause.

"But Daddy, it sounds just like I was talking about bread."

❖ ❖ ❖

REASON ENOUGH

Bobby sat on his front steps looking very blue. His best chum saw him and shouted from across the street to come play ball. Bobby shook his head despondently and then Billy crossed the street to see what was wrong.

" Say, what's the matter with you, Bob — you don't look right."

" Aw, my collie died."

" He did? Say that's too bad; but gosh there ain't no use cryin' over it. Why my grandmother died last week but I didn't cry."

" Yes, but you didn't raise your grandmother from a pup like I did."

JOHNNY'S PENNY

Johnny had been sent to the store and given a penny for himself. When he returned the tears were streaming down his face.

" Why, what is the matter, Johnny? " asked his mother.

" It's m' penny! "

" What happened — did you lose it? "

" No'm, I swallered it! "

" You swallowed your penny! Come, Johnny, we must go to Doctor James at once."

" I don't want to go the doctor's. I want to go to the minister's."

" But Johnny, why do you want to go to the minister's? "

" Cause m' Uncle Bob said that the minister was the only person 'at could get any money out of you! "

HOW GIRLS STUDY

Did you ever see two girls get together to study of an evening? I have, and it generally goes like this:

In 1673 Marquette discovered the Mississippi. In 1673 Marquette dis — what did you say, Jane, you had ever so much rather have a long bob than a shingle? — Yes, I would too. It's so much more stylish, but how do you like — Oh! dear I can never learn this lesson!

In 1863 Lafayette discovered the Wisconsin. In 1863 Lafayette discovered the — well! what's the matter with me, anyhow! In 1673 Marquette discovered the Mississippi. I don't care if he did. I suppose the Mississippi would have gotten along just as well if Marquette had never looked at it. Now, see here, Jane, is there anything about my looks that would give you to understand that I know when Columbus founded Jamestown, and how George Washington won the battle of Shiloh? Of course there isn't. History's a horrid study anyhow. No use neither. Now, French is much nicer. I can introduce French phrases very often, and every one must know I have studied the language. What is the lesson for to-morrow? Oh, yes, conjugation of parler. Let's see; how does it commence? Je parle, tu parle, il, par — il pa — il — well, il then!

" Conjugations don't amount to anything. I know some phrases that are appropriate here and there, and in almost every locality; and how's anybody going to know but what I have the conjugations all by heart?

" Have I got my geometry? No, I'm just going to study it. Thirty-ninth, is it not?

" Let the triangle A B C, triangle A B — say, Jane have you read the story in the World?

" Oh! theorem.

" Let the triangle A B C be right-angled at B. On the side B C, erect the square A I. On the side — did I tell you Sister Carracciola gave me a new piece to-day, a sonata? It is really intense. The tones fairly stir my soul. I am never going to take anything but sonatas after this.

I got another new piece, too. Its name is Études. Isn't it funny? I asked Tom this noon what it means and he says it is Greek for nothing. It is quite apropos, for there is really nothing in it — the same thing over and over.

"Where was I? Oh yes — side A C the Square A E. Draw the line — come on, let's go at our astronomy. Are the planets inhabited? Now, Jane I think they are, and I have thought about it a great deal. Yes, I cut my hair last night. Yes, I think they are inhabited. I should like to visit some of them, but you would not catch me living in Venus. Eight seasons! Just think how often we would have to have new outfits to keep up with the styles.

"What! you are not going? I am so sorry, but I suppose you are tired. I am. It always makes me most sick to study a whole evening like this. I think Sister ought to give us a picture."

And they go to school next morning and tell the other girls how awfully hard they have studied.

BELLE MC DONALD

❖   ❖   ❖

THE DAY OF JUDGMENT

I am thirteen years old and Jill is eleven and a quarter. Jill is my brother. That isn't his name, you know; his name is Timothy and mine is George Zacharias; but they call us Jack and Jill.

Well, Jill and I had an invitation to Aunt John's this summer, and that was how we happened to be there.

She'd invited us to come on the twelfth of August. It takes all day to get there. You have to wait at South Lawrence in a poky little depot, so we bought a paper and Jill read it. When he'd sat a minute and read along —

"Look here!" said he.

"Look where?" said I.

"Why there's going to be a comet," said Jill.

"Who cares?" said I.

Jill laid down the paper, and crunched a pop-corn all up before he answered that, then said he, "I don't see why father didn't tell us, I suppose he thought we'd be frightened, or something. Why, s'posing the world did come to an end? That's what this paper says. ' It is pre — ' where is my place? Oh! I see — ' predicted by learned men that a comet will come into con — conjunction with our plant ' — no — ' our planet this night. Whether we shall be plunged into a wild vortex of angry space, or suffocated with n-o-x — noxious gases, or scorched to a helpless crisp, or blasted at once, eternal an-ni-hi — ' " A gust of wind grabbed the paper out of Jill's hand just then, and took it out of the window; so I never heard the rest.

"Father isn't a goose," said I. "He didn't think it worth while mentioning. He isn't a-going to be afraid of a comet at his time of life." So we didn't think any more about the comet till we got to Aunt John's, where we found company. It wasn't a relation, only an old school friend, and her name was Miss Togy; she had to have the spare room because she was a lady. That was how Jill and I came to be put in the little chimney bed-room.

That little chimney bed-room is the funniest place you ever slept in. There had been a chimney once, and it ran up by the window, and grandfather had it taken away. It was a big, old-fashioned chimney, and it left the funniest little gouge in the room, so the bed went in as nice as could be. We couldn't see much but the ceiling when we got to bed.

"It's pretty dark," said Jill; "I shouldn't wonder if it did blow up a storm a little — wouldn't it scare — Miss Bogy!"

"Togy," said I.

"Well, T — o — " said Jill; and right in the middle of it he went off as sound as a weasel.

The next thing I can remember is a horrible noise. I can't think of but one thing in this world it was like, and that isn't in this world so much. I mean the last trumpet, with the angel blowing as he blows in my old primer. The next thing I remember is hearing Jill sit up in bed — for I couldn't see him, it was so dark — and his piping out the other half of Miss Togy's name just as he had left it when he went to sleep.

"Gy! — Bogy! — Fogy! — Soaky! — Oh! " said Jill, coming to at last, " I thought — why, what's up? "

I was up, but I couldn't tell what else was for a little while. I went to the window. It was as dark as a great rat-hole out-of-doors, all but a streak of lightning and an awful thunder, as if the world was cracking all to pieces.

I went back to bed, for I didn't know what else to do, and we crawled down under the clothes and covered ourselves all up.

"W — would — you — call — Aunt — John? " asked Jill. He was most choked. I came up for air.

"No," said I, " I don't think I'd call Aunt John." I should have liked to call her by that time, but then I should have felt ashamed.

"I s'pose she has got her hands full with Miss Croaky, anyway," chattered Jill, bobbing up and under again. By that time the storm was the worst storm I had ever seen in my life. It grew worse and worse — thunder, lightning, and wind — wind, lightning and thunder; rain and roar and awfulness. I don't know how to tell how awful it was.

In the middle of the biggest peal we'd had yet, up jumped Jill. " Jack! " said he, " That comet." I'd never thought of the comet till that minute: I felt an ugly feeling and cold all over. "It is the comet! " said Jill. " It is the day of judgment, Jack."

Then it happened. It happened so fast I didn't even have time to get my head under the clothes. First there was a creak, then a crash, then we felt a shake as if a giant pushed his shoulder up through the floor and shoved us. Then we doubled up. And then we began to fall. The floor opened, and we went through. I heard the bed-post hit as we went by. Then I felt another crash; then we began to fall again; then we bumped down hard. After that we stopped falling. I lay still. My heels were doubled up over my head. I thought my neck would break. But I never dared to stir, for I thought I was dead. By and by I wondered if Jill were not dead too, so I undoubled my neck a little and found some air. It seemed just as uncomfortable to breathe without air when you were dead as when you weren't.

I called out softly, " Jill! " no answer. " Jill! " not a sound. " O — Jill! " But he did not speak, so then I knew Jill must be dead, at any rate. I couldn't help wondering why he was so much deader than I that he couldn't answer a fellow. Pretty soon I heard a rustling noise around my feet, then a weak, sick kind of a voice, just the kind of noise I always supposed ghosts would make if they could talk.

" Jack? "

" Is that you, Jill? "

" I — suppose — so. Is it you, Jack? "

" Yes. Are you dead? "

" I don't know. Are you? "

" I guess I must be if you are. How awfully dark it is."

" Awfully dark! It must have been the comet."

" Yes; did you get much hurt? "

" Not much — I say, Jack? "

" What? "

" It is the judgment day."

Jill broke up, so did I; we lay as still as we could. If it were the judgment day — " Jill! " said I.

" Oh, dear me! " sobbed Jill.

We were both crying by that time, and I don't feel ashamed to own up, either.

" If I'd known," said I, " that the day of judgment was coming on the 12th of August, I wouldn't have been so mean about that jack-knife of yours with the notch in it."

" And I wouldn't have eaten your lunch that day last winter when I got mad at you," said Jill.

" Nor we wouldn't have cheated mother about smoking, vacations," said I.

" I'd never have played with the Bailey boys out behind the barn," said Jill.

" I wonder where the comet went to? " said I.

" ' Whether we shall be plunged into,' " quoted Jill, in a horrible whisper, from that dreadful newspaper, " ' shall be plunged into a wild vortex of angry space — or suffocated with noxious gases — or scorched into a helpless crisp — or blasted — ' "

" When do you think they will come after us? " I interrupted Jill.

That very minute somebody came. We heard a step and then another, then a heavy bang. Jill howled out a little. I didn't, for I was thinking how the cellar door banged like that. Then came a voice, an awful hoarse and trembling voice as ever you heard.

" George Zacharias! "

Then I knew it must be the judgment day and that the angel had me in court to answer him, for you couldn't expect an angel to call you Jack after you was dead.

" George Zacharias! " said the awful voice again. I didn't know what else to do, I was so frightened, so I just hollered out, " Here! " as I do in school.

" Timothy! " came the voice once more.

Now Jill had a bright idea. Up he shouted, " Absent! " at the top of his lungs.

" George! Jack! Jill! Where are you? Are you killed? Oh, wait a minute, and I'll bring a light."

This didn't sound so much like judgment day as it did like Aunt John. I began to feel better. So did Jill. I sat up. So did he. It wasn't a minute till the light came into sight, and something that looked like a cellar door, the cellar steps, and Aunt John's spotted wrapper, and Miss Togy in a night-gown, away behind as white as a ghost. Aunt John held the light above her head and looked down. I don't believe I shall ever see an angel that will make me feel any better to look at than Aunt John did that night.

" O you blessed boys! " said Aunt John — she was laughing and crying together. " To think that you should have fallen through the old chimney to the cellar floor and be sitting there alive in such a funny heap as that! "

And that was just what we had done. The old flooring (not very secure) had given away in the storm; and we'd gone down through two stories, where the chimney ought to have been, jam! into the cellar on the coal heap, and all as good as ever excepting the bedstead.

ELIZABETH STUART PHELPS

✿ ✿ ✿ ✿ ✿ ✿ ✿ ✿ ✿ ✿

POEMS FOR
HOLIDAY OCCASIONS

THE NEW LEAF

He came to my desk with quivering lip,
The lesson was done.
" Have you a new leaf for me, dear Teacher?
I have spoiled this one! "
I took his leaf, all soiled and blotted
And gave him a new one, all unspotted,
Then into his tired heart I smiled:
" Do better now, my Child! "

I went to the throne, with trembling heart.
The year was done.
" Have you a New Year for me, dear Master?
I have spoiled this one! "
He took my year, all soiled and blotted
And gave me a new one all unspotted,
Then into my tired heart he smiled:
" Do better now, my Child! "

❖　❖　❖

IN A STABLE

The little baby calf that lay
Beside its mother in the hay,
Didn't it have a word to say
When little Jesus came to stay?

The baby lamb within the stall,
Didn't it cry at all?

That little calf, it held its breath,
The little lamb was still as death,
They did not even whisper, lest
The baby cry at Mary's breast.

When Jesus came into the stall
They made no sound at all.

VIRGINIA WOODS MACKALL

❖ ❖ ❖

A TELEPHONE CONVERSATION
The day after Christmas

" Oh! Hello Elsie!
Is that you?
Glad you called me up.
What? Christmas!
Yes, we had a nice enough time.
What did I get?
Oh, the usual things.
Of course I had a good time!
I don't sound so?
Well, what of that?
You can't be gay
Every blessed minute of the day
Even if it is the merry Christmastide.
What did the family give me?
Let me see.
Oh yes, Daddy gave me a fur coat —
Beaver, of course, —
A wrist-watch,
And a desk (Colonial style);
Mother?
Glove-silk underwear
And a set of jade — earings, necklace and bracelet to
match.
I'm lucky!
Well perhaps I am.
Is that all?

Oh well I got the usual things of course —
Silk stockings, gloves, handkerchiefs — (Suddenly remembers)
Oh thank you for the dance handkerchief.
It's the *sweetest* thing,
Just what I wanted —
So kind of you to remember.
What did you say?
The Russian wolf-hound
Uncle John promised me?
Yes, he's here all right.
His name?
Boris I guess, or Ivan or one of those Russian names.

Just a minute, there's the bell."

    (returns with letter in her hand — tears it open, reads with mounting interest and ecstatically grabs the telephone)

" Elsie! Elsie! What do you think?
I've just received the most *bee-uu-ti-ful* Christmas *card* from Jack! "

LUCY VAUGHN ENOCH

❖ ❖ ❖

JOYOUS CHRISTMAS

Now's the gladdest time to give;
And the sweetest time to live;
Now's the time for holy joy.

Now's the liltful time to sing;
And the blessed time to bring,
Praise to God, without alloy.

Now's the safest time to spend;
Fittest time a gift to send,
To the needy, poor man's door.

Give the very best you own;
Live as Christ the Lord hath shown;
Sing!   But love a little more!

Now's a time devout, to pray;
And the Spirit's time to say;
" Lord, I love Thee, and adore."

JOHN GRANT NEWMAN

❖   ❖   ❖

TWINS

Polly speaks

There's such a lot that Santa Claus
    Must 'tend to when he b'gins,
I feel a little anxious, 'cause
    He might forget we're twins.

S'posin' he'd peek in at our bed
    'Bout 'leven or half-past ten,
And say, " There's Dolly Brooks's head,
    And — Dolly Brooks again! "

And then he'd pull our stockings down
    And shake his head, and say,
With such a dreadful angry frown,
    " She can't fool me that way! "

Dolly speaks

Poor Polly wouldn't have a thing.
    How terr'ble that would be!
For every single toy he'd bring
    He'd s'pose would b'long to me.

Polly! let's take our picture-books
    Before we go to bed,
Marked " Polly Brooks " and " Dolly Brooks,"
    And hang them overhead.

Then when old Santa comes our way,
    He'll smile the biggest grins,
And tiptoe 'round the bed, and say,
    " What have we here?   Ah, twins! "

CAROLINE E. CONDIT

❖ ❖ ❖

THE THREE KINGS

Three kings came riding from far away,
    Melchior and Gaspar and Baltasar;
Three Wise Men out of the East were they,
And they travelled by night and they slept by day,
    For their guide was a beautiful, wonderful star.

The star was so beautiful, large and clear,
    That all the other stars of the sky
Became a white mist in the atmosphere,
And by this they knew that the coming was near
    Of the Prince, foretold in the prophecy.

Three caskets they bore on their saddle-bows,
    Three caskets of gold with golden keys;
Their robes were of crimson silk with rows
Of bells and pomegranates and furbelows
    Their turbans like blossoming almond trees.

And so the Three Kings rode into the West,
    Through the dusk of night, over hill and dell,
And sometimes they nodded with beard on breast,
And sometimes talked, as they paused to rest,
    With the people they met at some wayside well.

" Of the child that is born," said Baltasar,
   " Good people, I pray you, tell us the news;
For we in the East have seen his star,
And have ridden fast, and have ridden far,
   To find and worship the King of the Jews."

And the people answered, " You ask in vain;
   We know of no king but Herod the Great! "
They thought the Wise Men were men insane,
As they spurred their horses across the plain,
   Like riders in haste, and who cannot wait.

And when they came to Jerusalem,
   Herod the Great, who had heard this thing,
Sent for the Wise Men and questioned them;
And said, " Go down unto Bethlehem,
   And bring me tidings of this new king."

So they rode away; and the star stood still,
   The only one in the gray of morn;
Yes, it stopped, it stood still of its own free will,
Right over Bethlehem on the hill,
   The city of David where Christ was born.

And the Three Kings rode through the gate and the guard,
   Through the silent street, till their horses turned
And neighed as they entered the great inn-yard;
But the windows were closed and the doors were barred,
   And only a light in the stable burned.

And cradled there in the scented hay,
   In the air made sweet by the breath of kine,
The little child in the manger lay,
The child, that would be king one day
   Of a kingdom not human but divine.

His mother Mary of Nazareth
    Sat watching beside his place of rest,
Watching the even flow of his breath,
For the joy of life and the terror of death
    Were mingled together in her breast.

They laid their offerings at his feet:
    The gold was their tribute to a King,
The frankincense, with its odor sweet,
Was for the Priest the Paraclete,
    The myrrh for the body's burying.

And the mother wondered and bowed her head,
    And sat as still as a statue of stone;
Her heart was troubled yet comforted,
Remembering what the Angel had said
    Of an endless reign and of David's throne.

Then the Kings rode out of the city gate,
    With a clatter of hoofs in proud array;
But they went not back to Herod the Great,
For they knew his malice and feared his hate,
    And returned to their homes by another way.

HENRY W. LONGFELLOW

❖ ❖ ❖

THE GINGERBREAD HORSE

A maid from Japan and a little toy man,
Sat with other toys under the tree.
Said the little toy man to the maid from Japan
" Will you come on a journey with me?
We will travel of course, on this gingerbread horse;
He's a dear and you must understand,
He can run; he can fly; he will take you and I
In a jiffy to Make Believe Land.

" We will see Jack and Jill on the very same hill
On which Jack once had a bad bump;
We will try to find out, just to settle all doubt,
What his Mother rubbed into the lump.
We'll see the Old Woman who lived in a shoe —
Find out if the gossip about her is true.

" We will call on King Cole, that merrie old soul,
And find out if we possibly can,
What his fiddlers did play when they charmed him that day,
He must be a funny old man.
We'll see Jackie Horner's most wonderful thumb
And ask him to tell what he did with his plum.

" Dear little Bo Peep who lost all her sheep
Was a flapper and she liked to roam;
But I'd like to know — we'll find out if it's so —
Did those sheep ever find their way home?
What kind of horn was it that little boy blew?
I think it's important to know this; don't you?

" Tonight would be fine for this journey of mine;
We can just slip away from these toys,
For tomorrow, of course, this dear gingerbread horse
Will be eaten by one of the boys."
Said the maid from Japan to the little toy man,
" To journey with you would be grand,
If you'll promise me true, that you'll marry me, too,
When we get to that Make Believe Land."

JAMES W. STANISTREET

THE NATIVITY

A Baby cried within a lowly stable,
"No room for them in all the inn."
A Baby born from God to man
To link that lost estate of man
Again to earth, as was God's plan.
A child's cry faint, a mother over-borne,
Strangers in a lowly homely place
Yet owning all the world as made by Him —
By Him, the lonely and so left alone.
But lo, on starry heights the angels sang
And shepherds sought the Baby's bed;
The wise men brought their gifts of gold
And frankincense and myrrh.
The oxen stall was changed to royal chamber.
The darkness, pain and gloom
Became illumined with a heavenly light,
Sweet music filled with adoration earth and air
    For God was there.

ELIZABETH LYMAN HARTLEY

❖ ❖ ❖

THE STRANGE CHILD'S CHRISTMAS

There went a stranger child,
    As Christmas Eve closed in,
Through the streets of a town, whose windows shone
    With the warmth and light within.

It stopped at every house
    The Christmas tree to see
On that festive night, when they shone so bright —
    And it sighed right bitterly.

[225]

Then wept the child, and said,
  " This night hath everyone
A Christmas tree, that he glad may be,
  And I alone have none.

"Will no one let me in?
  No presents would I crave,
But to see the light, and the tree all bright,
  And the gifts that others have.

" Mother and father are dead —
  O Jesus, kind and dear,
I've no one now, there is none but Thou,
  For I am forgotten here! "

But see — another Child
  Comes gliding through the street,
And its robe is white, in its hand a light;
  It speaks, and its voice is sweet.

" Once on this earth a Child
  I lived, as thou livest yet;
Though all turn away from thee today,
  Yet I will not forget.

" Here, in the darkness dim,
  I'll show thee, child, thy tree;
Those that spread their light through the chambers bright
  So lovely scarce can be."

And with its white hand points
  The Christ-child to the sky,
And lo! afar, with each lamp a star,
  A tree gleamed there on high.

So far, and yet so near,
  The light shone overhead;
And all was well, for the child could tell
  For whom that tree was spread.

It gazed as in a dream,
  And angels bent and smiled,
And with outstretched hand to that brighter land
  They carried the stranger child.

And the little one went home
  With its Saviour Christ to stay,
All hunger and cold and the pain of old
  Forgotten and passed away.

FROM THE GERMAN

❖ ❖ ❖

PENELOPE'S CHRISTMAS DANCE

Mistress Penelope Penwick, she,
Called by her father, " My sweet P,"
Painted by Peale, she won renown
In a clinging, short-waisted satin gown,
A red rose touched by her finger-tips,
And a smile held back from her roguish lips.
Thus William Penwick, the jolly wight,
In clouds of smoke, night after night,
Would tell a tale of delighted pride,
To cronies who came from far and wide,
Always ending, with candle he,
" And this is the picture of my sweet P! "

The tale? 'Twas how sweet P did chance
To give the British a Christmas dance.

Penwick's house past the outpost stood,
Flanked by the ferry and banked by the wood.
Hessian and British quartered there
Swarmed through chamber and hall and stair.
Fires ablaze and candles alight;
Soldier and officer feasted that night.
The enemy? Safe, with a river between,
Black and deadly and fierce and keen,
A river of ice and a blinding storm!
So they made them merry and kept them warm.
But while they mirth and roistering made,
Up in her dormer window stayed
Mistress Penelope Penwick apart,
With fearful thought and sorrowful heart.
Night by night had her candle's gleam
Sent through the night its hopeful beam.
But the nights they came and passed again
With never a sign from her countrymen.
For where beat the heart so brave, so bold
Which could baffle that river's bulwark cold?
Penelope's eyes and her candle's light
Were mocked by the storm that Christmas night.
But lo! full sudden a missile stung
And shattered her casement-pane and rung
At her feet! — 'Twas a word from the storm outside;
She opened her dormer window wide —
A wind-swept figure halted below —
The ferryman, old and bent and slow.
Then a murmur rose upward — only one,
Thrilling and powerful — " Washington! "
Hark! At that warning, magic word,
What was the sound Penelope heard,
Beyond the wind and the whirling snow,
Far and faint, and deep and low?
It was not the river rushing along,

[228]

It was not the roar of the Hessian song!
With jest and laughter, and candles bright,
'Twas two by the stairway clock that night
When Penelope Penwick tripped her down
Dressed in a short-waisted satin gown
With a red rose, (cut from her potted bush),
There fell on the rollicking crown a hush.
She stood in the soldier's midst, I ween,
The daintiest thing they e'er had seen!
And swept their gaze with her eyes most sweet,
And patted her little slippered feet;
" 'Tis Christmas night sirs," quoth sweet P.
"I should like to dance! Will you dance with me? "
Oh! but they cheered! Ran to and fro;
And each for the honor bowed him low.
With smiling charm and witching grace
She chose him pranked with officer's lace,
And shining buttons and dangling sword;
No doubt he strutted him proud as a lord!
Doffed was enmity, donned was glee.
Oh, she was charming, that sweet P!
And when it was over and blood aflame,
Came an eager cry for " A game, a game! "
" We'll play at forfeits," Penelope cried.
" If one holdeth aught in his love and pride,
Let each lay it down at my feet in turn
And a fine from me shall he straightway learn! "
What held they all in their love and pride?
Straight flew a hand to every side!
Each man had a sword and nothing more
And the swords they clanged in a heap on the floor.
Standing there in her satin gown,
With candlelight on her yellow crown
And at her feet a bank of steel,
(I'll wager that look was caught by Peale)

Penelope held her rose on high —
" I fine ye each for a leaf to try! "
She plucked the petals and blew them out,
A rain of red they fluttered about
Over the floor and through the air —
Rushed the officers here and there —
When lo! a cry!   The door burst in!
" The enemy! "   Tumult, terror and din!
Flew a hand unto every side —
Swords?   Penelope, arms thrown wide
Leapt that heap of steel before,
Swords behind her on the floor,
Facing her countrymen staunch and bold
Who dared the river of death and cold
Who swept them down on a rollicking horde
And found them never a man with a sword!

And so it happened (but not by chance)
In '76 there was given a dance
By a witch with a rose and a satin gown
(Painted in Philadelphia-town),
Mistress Penelope Penwick she,
Called by her father, " My sweet P."

                    VIRGINIA WOODWARD CLOUD

❖   ❖   ❖

SANTA CLAUS IN THE TRENCHES

The sky was blue-blue
And the snow was white-white!
And the stars blazed like candles
St. Nicholas night
Near Altkirch town,
Across the sea.

[230]

A-guarding the walls
Sat soldiers three;
They gazed at the campfires
And thought of the toys
Old Santa had brought to them
When they were boys.
The soldiers three
Had naught to say,
They were thinking
" Tomorrow is Christmas Day
And home is far and far away! "
They looked — each one —
At the Christmas star,
And far away seemed very far!
The soldiers three
Had naught to say,
For they would be fighting
On Christmas Day.
The town clock struck —
Till sudden-up over the crest
The crest of the hill
Came a whirl of snow,
A trampling of feet,
A rattle of guns,
And the drums low beat!
At least — so it seemed
To the soldiers three.
They jumped to their feet —
" The enemy! "
Cries the first. " Halt! Hands up!
Who goes there? "
The words rang sharp in the crisp night air.
" Call the general! "
" Rouse the town! "
" Out upon 'em and

Shoot 'em down! "
The whirl of snow
Came nearer — then stopped
Out of the mist
An old man hopped.
" Hands up!   Hands up! "
Cried the soldiers three,
" Hands up or we shoot —
Who'er you be! "
" Why, boys!   Why boys!
Don't you know me?
Why I'm old St. Nicholas,
Can't you see?
Why hello John!
Why hello Jack!
And Jim, my boy —
Put that gun back! "
The soldiers three
Had naught to say,
They stared at St. Nick —
They stared at the sleigh!
The rattling of guns?
'Twas the toys in the sack
That jolly St. Nicholas
Had on his back.
The drums! the drums!
The drums low beat!
'Twas the prancing, dancing
Reindeer feet!
" Come, hurry and give me
A pass, my boys —
A pass for St. Nick
And his load of toys
For I must be off
And be up and away —

I've millions of children to see
Before day."
And while he waited
He read out the list
Of children good,
So that none would be missed.
" Are our names there? "
Cried the soldiers three —
" You know St. Nick
They used to be."
" When boys grow up
And go to war
They are not good boys
Any more! "
Old Santa called,
Jumped into his sleigh.
They gave him the pass
And away — away —
Up over the walls
To the chimneys red
Rose St. Nick and his pack
And his wonderful sled!
But what do you think?
The soldiers three
Found their boots
As full as could be
Of candy and lollypops
Jack-knives and toys
And all of the things
They'd loved as boys!
" I wish," said a note
From St. Nick, " that you
Would forget tonight
That you're soldiers — do!
'orget tonight that you're

Grown up men —
Pretend you're my own
Little boys again.
The John and Jack
That I used to know
The Jim who wrote to me
Long ago! "
And that is the tale
As 'twas told to me
Of what happened in Altkirch
To the soldiers three.

❖ ❖ ❖

THE ENCHANTED OAK

Beneathe an ancient oake one daye
A holye friar kneeled to praye.
Scarce had he mumbled Aves three
When lo! a voice within the tree
Straighte to the friar's hearte it wente.
A voice as of some spirit pente
Within the hollow of the tree
That cried, " Good father, sette me free."

Quothe he, " This hath an evil sounde
Ande bent him lower to the grounde.
But ever tho' he prayed, the more
The voice hys pytie didde implore,
Untyl he raised hys eyes and there
Beheld a mayden ghostlie faire.
Thus to the holye manne she spoke:

" Within the hollowe of this oake
Enchanted for a hundred yeares,

Have I been bounde — yette vain my teares!
Notte anything can breake the banne
Till I be kissed by holye manne."

"Woe's me," thenne sayd the friar, " If thou
Be sente to tempt me breake my vowe,
Butte whether mayde or fiende thou be,
I'll stake my soul to sette thee free."
The holye manne then crossed hym thrice
And kissed the mayde — when in a trice
She vanished. " Heaven forgive me now,"
Exclaimed the friar, " my broken vowe!

" If I have sinned, I sinned to save
Another fromme a living grave."
Thenne downe upon the earth he felle,
And prayed some sign that he might telle
If he were doomed evermore;
When lo! the oake alle bare before
Put forth a brance of palest greene,
And fruited everywhere betweene
With waxen berries, pearlie white,
A miracle before hys sight.

*   *   *   *   *   *

The holye friar wente hys waye
And told hys tale. And from thatte daye
It hath been writ that anye manne
May blameless kiss what mayde he canne;
Nor anyone shall say hym " no,"
Beneath the holye mistletoe.

OLIVER HERFORD

THE LEGEND OF THE HAWTHORN'S
CHRISTMAS BLOOM

Led by some need that rules their little world,
Men wend their steps afar
And for a while may make of fame or gain
Their spirit's guiding star.

But as the circle of the months rolls 'round,
No matter where they roam,
When Christmas comes they hear the still small voice
That sweetly sings of home.

An aged legend, grey with passing years,
Tells us of Joseph. He
Who tombward bore the body of the Lord
When from the cross set free.

His work accomplished in the Holy Land,
He sped across the wave
To Britain's isle and preached the Word of God
To sanctify and save.

And whereso'er his duty bade him tend,
His feet were swift to go.
Fierce summer's heat was nothing to his zeal
And nothing winter's snow.
Come darkest night with terror in its train —
Come weary lengths to stray —
As light as lark that greets the morning sun
He started on his way.

So, as he wandered on his varied path,
By plain and country-side,
It happened he came to Glastonbury's Hill
Around the Christmastide.

[236]

"I'll wait," he said, and upright by his side
He thrust his good staff strong.
Thus placed that ready for his grasp 'twould mean
He should not rest too long.

The people came. He spoke to them of Him
Who died upon a tree,
Who shed his blood to put an end to sin
That mankind might be free.
They, deeply moved, with warm words welcome him,
Nor did he thence depart
Till signs of promise from the seed he'd sown
Had sprung in every heart.

Rejoiced, exalted, upward borne by prayer,
So joyous in his mind —
In faith made stronger — he set forth once more —
But left his staff behind.
So fair a field was this where he had tilled,
So rich in hopeful grain,
He quite o'erlooked the burden of his years
And had grown young again.

But as is oft the custom of the world,
Ere many moons had fled,
They seek return into their former ways —
The idols they had wed.
Forgot their promise fair —
A change but builded out of ocean's sand,
Repentance writ in air.

A pall of white — a winding sheet of snow —
Hides Nature's winter face,
As out they crowd to Glastonbury Hill
For revels not of grace.

When, lo! They note with wonder and amaze
The staff of hawthorn fair
Left by the Saint had sudden burst to bloom
In flowered glory there.

He's then remembered. Then their minds recall
A year ago this day,
With all between. And as the truth comes back,
They pause a while to pray.
Another spirit enters in their song;
Their wild carousings cease,
As sweeter pleasures flood them with their joys
Along with love and peace.

Forever after as the cycles rolled
The dying years away,
The staff, now tree-grown, always bloomed the same
On Holy Christmas Day.
It bloomed in spite of frost and keenest blast,
In spite of winter's cold,
It had a tale to tell of Heaven's love
And thus its tale was told.

So runs the story. Whatsoe'er we are,
Wherever we may be,
Our hearts are like Saint Joseph's hawthorn staff
That blossomed to a tree.
We may forget, wrapped up in worldly thought,
Or sometimes careless stray,
But love's stout staff stands fixed in every heart
And blooms on Christmas Day.

P. H. DOYLE

CAROL

We saw him sleeping in his manger bed,
And falter'd feet and heart in holy dread
Until we heard the maiden mother call:
Come hither, sirs, he is so sweet and small.

She was more fair than ye have look'd upon,
She was the moon, and he her little sun;
O Lord, we cry'd, have mercy on us all!
But ah, quod she, he is so sweet and small.

Whereat the blessed beasts with one accord
Gave tongue to praise their little Lord,
Oxen and asses singing in their stall;
The king of kings he is so sweet and small.

GERALD BULLETT

❖ ❖ ❖

WHAT CAN I GIVE HIM?

What can I give Him
    Poor as I am?
If I were a shepherd
    I would bring Him a lamb.
If I were a wise man
    I would do my part, —
Yet what can I give Him?
    Give my heart.

CHRISTINA G. ROSSETTI

❖ ❖ ❖

SPOOKS

Once while walking through the woods
On a moonless, starless night,
I tried to believe there were no spooks
    Hidden out of sight.

[239]

I turned and looked about me —
To my left and to my right.
When I saw a long hand pointing,
    That made me cold with fright.

I looked at it intently
Till I could plainly see
That it wasn't any spook at all,
    But an ordinary tree.

I hadn't walked much farther
When I sudd'nly stood still
For I heard a weird uncanny sound
    That filled me with a chill.

I walked a little farther
For I found it was an owl
And I scolded myself for being scared
    By such a harmless fowl.

I tried to keep my spirits up
By singing a merry tune
When rising up above the trees
    I saw the bright new moon.

It filled me with a gladness
That I could not well restrain.
For I knew now I would not be
    Scared by spooks again.

            HENRIETTA WEISS (15 years)

THE GOBLIN

Once in the darkest part of the night
    I wakened, scared as could be,
A dreadful something crouched by my bed
    And seemed to be watching me.
One arm was raised, the head was bowed
    Its form was twisted and queer
When I called " Mother " shaky but loud
    I hoped it would disappear.
But grin it would as Mother laughed low
    Then sent high the window shade.
The moonlight showed what had tricked me so
    I'm ashamed to have been afraid.

Can you believe that a parasol
    I had dropped so carelessly there
With my coat and tam and basket ball
    Could have given me such a scare?
Since then I've been as neat as can be
    More careful than ever before
For having clothes goblins call on me
    Is something I wish no more.

BESSIE STONE WARING

❖ ❖ ❖

ON HALLOWE'EN

On Hallowe'en an old witch flies
Upon a broomstick through the skies
'N' gleaming goblins dressed in white
Go sliding gliding through the night

'N' big black bats with big black wings
Go flop against the walls an' things
'N' round eyed owls cry " Who-who-who "
But — I'm not scared a bit, are you?

ELSIE FOWLER

❖   ❖   ❖

THANKSGIVING DAY

Most folks like Thanksgiving Day
But like it in a different way than me.
Bud thinks of turkey and pumpkin pie
And how he'll make the goodies fly.
But I like Thanksgiving Day
'Cause Christmas's just a month away.

LUCILLE MURRAY

❖   ❖   ❖

THANKSGIVING

I want to thank You first of all,
Dear God, for making me.
Because — if I had not been made —
Goodness! Where would I be?
And then I want to thank You, God,
For my dearest mother —
O! I'm glad I have her, God,
Instead of another!
And then I want to thank You for
My father and the boys,
And for my sisters, too, and for
Our house and for our toys!
And God, I want to thank You for
The lovely, lovely sky,

And for the clouds that way, way up
Above the world go by!
And God, I want to thank You for
The woods in which we play,
And for the stars and moon by night,
And for the sun by day . . .
And God, I want to thank You for
The daisy-fields and hills
Made to coast down in winter-time,
And have the finest spills!
And God, I want to thank You for
All sorts of little things —
Like curly stems of dandelions,
And pebbles, and the wings
Of butterflies, and icicles,
And leaves, and bugs that pass —
O! And for diamonds that I find
Each morning in the grass!
Dear God, there are a million things
To thank You for, I know!
I haven't thought of half of them —
For instance, there is snow . . .
But God, I don't believe I can
Remember all that I
Have got to thank You for, and so
I don't believe I'll try.
But God — You know the way I feel —
I mean I love You, and
O! Thank You just for everything!
There! Now you understand!

MARY DIXON THAYER

THE IVY GREEN

Oh, a dainty plant is the ivy green,
That creepeth o'er ruins old!
Of right choice food are his meals, I ween,
In his cell so lone and cold,
The wall must be crumbled, the stones decayed,
To pleasure his dainty whim;
And the mouldering dust that years have made
Is a merry meal for him,
Creeping where no life is seen,
A rare old plant is the ivy green.

Whole ages have fled and their words decayed
And nations have scattered before;
But the stout old ivy shall never fade,
From its hale and hearty green.
The brave old plant in its lonely days,
Shall fasten upon the past;
For the stateliest building man can raise,
Is the ivy's food at last,
Creeping on where time has been;
A rare old plant is the ivy green.

CHARLES DICKENS

❖   ❖   ❖

FOR ARBOR DAY

What do we do when we plant a tree?
We plant the ship which will cross the sea;
We plant the mast to carry the sails:
We plant the planks to withstand the gales —
The keel, keelson, and beam and knee —
We plant the ship when we plant the tree.

What do we do when we plant the tree?
We plant the house for you and me;
We plant the rafters, the shingles, the floors,
We plant the studding, the lath, the doors,
The beams, the siding, all parts that be;
We plant the home when we plant the tree.

What do we plant when we plant the tree?
A thousand things that we daily see;
We plant the spire that out-towers the crag,
We plant the staff for our country's flag,
We plant the shade from the hot sun free;
We plant all these when we plant the tree.

❖ ❖ ❖

THE STARS AND STRIPES

What nobleness, what glory you declare,
   What ideals typify!
Symbolic of friendship to mankind,
   Your banner lights the sky.

Red stripes! Assurance that before the brave
   Ignoble wrongs give way;
Emblem for all of opportunity,
   The dawning of a day.

White stripes! Recalling words of long ago,
   The pure their God shall see.
A wide-flung truth which all the world can prove
   Brings joy and liberty.

Blue field with stars of white! True brotherhood,
   The world in unity;
A pledge to all mankind of helpfulness
   And unselfed charity.

Your blended whole checks evil's forward march,
  And bids its hosts stand still;
You hold the promise of the world at peace,
  " To all mankind good will."

ARTHUR HOLLIS

❖   ❖   ❖

ABRAHAM LINCOLN

Such was he, our Martyr-Chief,
Whom late the Nation he had led,
With ashes on her head,
Wept with the passion of an angry grief:
Forgive me, if from present things I turn
To speak what in my heart will beat and burn,
And hang my wreath on his world-honored urn.
Nature, they say, doth dote,
And cannot make a man
Save on some worn-out plan,
Repeating us by rote:
For him her Old World moulds aside she threw,
And, choosing sweet clay from the breast
Of the unexhausted West,
With stuff untainted shaped a hero new,
Wise, steadfast in the strength of God, and true.
How beautiful to see
Once more a shepherd of mankind indeed,
Who loved his charge, but never loved to lead;
One whose meek flock the people joyed to be,
Not lured by any cheat of birth,
But by his clear-grained human worth,
And brave old wisdom of sincerity!
They knew that outward grace is dust;
They could not choose but trust
In that sure-footed mind's unfaltering skill,

And supple-tempered will
That bent like perfect steel to spring again and thrust.
His was no lonely mountain-peak of mind,
Thrusting to thin air o'er our cloudy bats,
A sea-mark now, now lost in vapors blind,
Broad prairie rather, genial, level-lined,
Fruitful and friendly for all human kind,
Yet also nigh to heaven and loved of loftiest stars.
Nothing of Europe here,
Or, then, of Europe fronting mornward still,
Ere any names of Serf and Peer
Could Nature's equal scheme deface;
Here was a type of the true elder race,
And one of Plutarch's men talked with us face to face.
I praise him not; it were too late;
And some innative weakness there must be
In him who condescends to victory
Such as the Present given, and cannot wait,
Safe in himself as in a fate.
So always firmly he:
He knew to bide his time
And can his fame abide,
Still patient in his simple faith sublime,
Till the wise years decide.
Great captains, with their guns and drums,
Disturb our judgment for the hour,
But at last silence comes;
These all are gone, and, standing like a tower,
Our children shall behold his fame,
The kindly-earnest, brave, foreseeing man,
Sagacious, patient, dreading praise, not blame,
New birth of our new soil, the first American.

JAMES RUSSELL LOWELL

GEORGE WASHINGTON

Soldier and statesman, rarest unison;
High-poised example of great duties done
Simply as breathing, a world's honors worn
As life's indifferent gifts to all men born;
Dumb for himself, unless it were to God,
But for his barefoot soldiers eloquent,
Tramping the snow to coral where they trod,
Held by his awe in Hollow-eyed content;
Modest, yet firm as Nature's self; unblamed
Save by the men his nobler temper shamed;
Never seduced through show of present good
By other than unsetting lights to steer
New-trimmed in Heaven, nor than his steadfast mood
More steadfast, far from rashness as from fear,
Rigid, but with himself first, grasping still
In swerveless poise the wave-beat helm of will;
Not honored then or now because he wooed
The popular voice, but that he still withstood;
Broadminded, higher-souled, there is but one
Who was all this and ours, and all men's — WASHINGTON.

JAMES RUSSELL LOWELL

❖ ❖ ❖

THE AMERICAN FLAG

When Freedom, from her mountain height,
Unfurl'd her standard to the air,
She tore the azure robe of night,
And set the stars of glory there!
She mingled with its gorgeous dyes
The milky baldric of the skies,
And striped its pure celestial white
With streakings of the morning light,

Then, from his mansion in the sun,
She call'd her eagle bearer down,
And gave into his mighty hand
The symbol of her chosen land!

Majestic monarch of the cloud!
Who rear'st aloft thy regal form,
To hear the tempest-trumpings loud,
And see the lightning lances driven,
When strive the warriors of the storm,
And rolls the thunder-drum of heaven —
Child of the Sun! to thee 'tis given
To guard the banner of the free.
To hover in the sulphur smoke,
To ward away the battle-stroke,
And bid its blendings shine afar,
Like rainbows on the cloud of war
The harbingers of victory!

Flag of the brave! thy folds shall fly,
The sign of hope and triumph high!
When speaks the signal-trumpet tone,
And the long line comes gleaming on,
Ere yet the life-blood, warm and wet,
Has dimm'd the glistening bayonet,
Each soldier's eyes shall brightly turn
To where the sky-born glories burn,
And as his springing steps advance,
Catch war and vengeance from the glance.
And when the cannon-mouthings loud
Heave in wild wreaths the battle shroud,
And gory sabres rise and fall
Like shoots of flame on midnight's pall,

Then shall thy meteor glances glow,
And cowering foes shall shrink beneath
Each gallant arm that strikes below
That lovely messenger of death.

Flag of the seas! on ocean wave
Thy stars shall glitter o'er the brave;
When death, careering on the gale,
Sweeps darkly round the bellied sail,
And frighted waves rush wildly back
Before the broadside's reeling rack,
Each dying wanderer of the sea
Shall look at once to heaven and thee,
And smile to see thy splendors fly
In triumph o'er his closing eye.
Flag of the free heart's hope and home,
By angel-hands to valor given,
Thy stars have lit the welkin dome,
And all thy hues were born in heaven,
Forever float that standard sheet,
Where breathes the foe but falls before us,
With Freedom's soil beneath our feet,
And Freedom's banner streaming o'er us!

JOSEPH RODMAN DRAKE

*** ✿ ✿ ✿ ✿ ✿ ✿ ✿ ✿ ✿ ✿***

POEMS TO COSTUME

DAS KLEINE KIND

Dare's a fairy comes und leads him
   Down der lane to Drowsytown,
Und der night yust in his honor
   Vares his fery bestest gown,
Und der boys vot lif in dreamland
   All come oud to take a peep,
Ven das kleine Kind is blinking,
        Vinking,
        Sinking,
        Into sleep.

All der road is filled mit blossoms
   From der flowers uf Forget;
Und der stars dey visper ad him;
   " Ve vas here, alretty, yet.
Und undil der daylights dawning
   Over you a vatch ve'll keep — "
Ven das kleine Kind is blinking,
        Vinking,
        Sinking,
        Into sleep.

Den dot fairy dells him stories
   Vot is mossic, vild und free;
Un dey fload on vare der moonlight
   Makes a soft und silfery sea;
Vile der vaves of sveet condentment
   All arount dem dance und leap —
Ven das kleine Kind is blinking,
        Vinking,
        Sinking,
        Into sleep.

Den dot fairy leads him through der
   Gates uf Drowsytown to vare
All der Poppy Children greet him
   At der place called Shut-eye Sqvare;
Den togedder mit each udder
   All der secrets do dey keep —
Und das kleine Kind stops blinking,
          Vinking,
          Sinking,
          Fast sleep.

GEORGE V. HOBART

❖   ❖   ❖

A BRAVE LITTLE QUAKERESS

It was in the winter of 1777, when the British army occupied Philadelphia, requisitioning houses as though by right.

Officers occupied the home of General Cadwalader — across Second Street from the home of Lydia Darrah. On occasion they had demanded the use of a room in the Darrah home for conferences. On December second, an officer told Lydia — called by her first name because she was a Quakeress — that a room in her house was required for conference that night; that she should have all her family abed by eight o'clock and that she would be notified when the conference ended so that she could extinguish the fire and put out the lights.

Unable to sleep while she feared her country was being plotted against, she crept to the door of the conference room and heard a plan outlined to make a night attack on General Washington's army encamped from White Marsh to Fort Washington.

Quietly regaining her room, she feigned sleep, and the officer called three times before " arousing her to close the house."

Next morning she told her husband she would ask passage of the British lines, that she might go to Frankford for flour. He insisted that their maid go along, but she feared to share her secret lest harm come to her home.

Off she started with a bag of wheat to be ground, through a light snow, toward the American lines, but was met by a detachment under General Boudinot. Asking to have a word with him she disclosed the British plans and in the journal of General Boudinot we find that it was he who finally delivered her message to General Washington.

The British, under General Howe did make the attack but the Colonial Army, forewarned, beat off three attacks and the British returned to Philadelphia, convinced that Washington had become acquainted with their plans and they wondered how the plot had leaked out. " Couldn't have been through the Darrahs, for the family was asleep before our conference began and I had to call Lydia three times when we were ready to leave."

And so a brave little Quakeress averted an American defeat.

❖   ❖   ❖

THE LITTLE QUAKER SINNER

A little Quaker maiden, with dimpled cheek and chin,
Before an ancient mirror stood, and viewed her from within.
She wore a gown of sober gray, a cape demure and prim,
With only simple fold and hem, yet dainty, neat, and trim.
Her bonnet, too, was gray and stiff; its only line of grace
Was in the lace, so soft and white, shirred round her rosy
    face.

Quoth she: " Oh, how I hate this hat! I hate this gown
    and cape!
I do wish all my clothes were not of such outlandish shape!

The children passing by to school have ribbons on their
　　hair;
The little girl next door wears red; oh, dear, if I could dare,
I know what I should like to do! "— (The words were
　　whispered low,
Lest such tremendous heresy should reach her aunts below.)

Calmly reading in the parlor sat the good aunts, Faith and
　　Peace,
Little dreaming how rebellious throbbed the heart of their
　　young niece.
All their prudent, humble teaching willfully she cast aside,
And, her mind now fully conquered by vanity and pride,
She, with trembling heart and fingers, on a hassock sat her
　　down,
And this little Quaker sinner sewed a tuck into her gown!

" Little Patience, art thou ready?　Fifth day meeting time
　　has come,
Mercy Jones and Goodman Elder with his wife have left
　　their home."
'Twas Aunt Faith's sweet voice that called her, and the
　　naughty little maid —
Gliding down the dark old stairway — hoped their notice to
　　evade,
Keeping shyly in their shadow as they went out at the door,
Ah! never little Quakeress a guiltier conscience bore!

Dear Aunt Faith walked looking upward; all her thoughts
　　were pure and holy;
And Aunt Peace walked gazing downward, with a humble
　　mind and lowly.
But " tuck — tuck! " chirped the sparrows, at the little
　　maiden's side;

And, in passing Farmer Watson's, where the barn-door
     opened wide,
Every sound that issued from it, every grunt and every
     cluck,
Was to her affrighted fancy like " a tuck! " " a tuck! "
     " a tuck! "

In meeting, Goodman Elder spoke of pride and vanity,
While all the Friends seemed looking round that dreadful
     tuck to see.
How it swelled in its proportions, till it seemed to fill the
     air,
And the heart of little Patience grew heavier with her care.
O, the glad relief to her, when, prayers and exhortations
     ended,
Behind her two good aunties her homeward way she wended!

The pomps and vanities of life she'd seized with eager arms,
And deeply she had tasted of the world's alluring charms —
Yea, to the dregs had drained them, and only this to find;
All was vanity of spirit and vexation of the mind.
So repentant, saddened, humbled, on her hassock she sat
     down,
And this little Quaker sinner ripped the tuck out of her
     gown!

LUCY MONTGOMERY

❖ ❖ ❖

THE FAIRIES OF THE CALDON-LOW

" And where have you been, my Mary,
     And where have you been from me? "
" I've been to the top of the Caldon-Low,
     The midsummer night to see! "

" And what did you see, my Mary,
    All up on the Caldon-Low? "
" I saw the blithe sunshine come down,
    And I saw the merry winds blow."

" And what did you hear, my Mary,
    All up on the Caldon Hill? "
" I heard the drops of the water made,
    And I heard the corn-ears fill."

" Oh, tell me all, my Mary —
    All, all that ever you know;
For you must have seen the fairies
    Last night on the Caldon-Low."

" Then take me on your knee, Mother,
    And listen, mother of mine;
A hundred fairies danced last night,
    And the harpers they were nine;

" And merry was the glee of the harp-strings,
    And their dancing feet so small;
But oh, the sound of their talking
    Was merrier far than all! "

" And what were the words, my Mary,
    That you did hear them say? "
" I'll tell you all, my Mother,
    But let me have my way.

" And some they played with the water,
    And rolled it down the hill;
' And this,' they said, ' shall speedily turn
    The poor old miller's mill;

"' For there has been no water
  Ever since the first of May;
And a busy man shall the miller be
  By the dawning of the day!

"' Oh, the miller, how he will laugh,
  When he sees the mill-dam rise!
The jolly miller, how he will laugh
  Till the tears fill both his eyes! '

" And some they seized the little winds,
  That sounded over the hill,
And each put a horn into his mouth,
  And blew so sharp and shrill: —

"' And there,' said they, ' the merry winds go
  Away from every horn;
And those shall clear the mildew dank
  From the blind old widow's corn.

"' Oh, the poor blind widow —
  Though she has been blind so long,
She'll be merry enough when the mildew's gone,
  And the corn stands stiff and strong! '

" And some they brought the brown linseed,
  And flung it down from the Low;
' And this,' said they, ' by the sunrise,
  In the weaver's croft shall grow!

"' Oh the poor lame weaver!
  How he will laugh outright
When he sees his dwindling flax-field
  All full of flowers by night! '

" And then up spoke a brownie,
  With a long beard on his chin;
' I have spun up all the tow,' said he,
  ' And I want some more to spin.

" ' I've spun a piece of hempen cloth,
  And I want to spin another —
A little sheet for Mary's bed,
  And an apron for her Mother! '

" And with that I could not help but laugh,
  And I laughed out loud and free;
And then on top of the Caldon-Low
  There was no one left but me.

" And all on top of the Caldon-Low
  The mists were cold and gray,
And nothing I saw but the mossy stones
  That round about me lay.

" But, as I came down from the hill-top,
  I heard, afar below,
How busy the jolly miller was,
  And how merry the wheel did go.

" And I peeped into the widow's field,
  And sure enough were seen
The yellow ears of the mildewed corn
  All standing stiff and green!

" And down by the weaver's croft I stole,
  To see if the flax were high;
But I saw the weaver at his gate,
  With the good news in his eye!

"Now this is all I heard, Mother,
    And all that I did see;
So, prithee, make my bed, Mother,
    For I'm tired as I can be!"

MARY HOWITT

❖ ❖ ❖

THE RAG DOLLY'S VALENTINE

Though others think I stare with eyes unseeing,
    I've loved you, Mistress mine, so dear to me,
With all my fervent rag-and-sawdust being
    Since first you took me from the Christmas Tree.
I love you though my only frock you tear off;
    I love you though you smear my face at meals;
I love you though you've washed my painted hair off;
    I love you when you drag me by the heels;
I love you though you've sewed three buttons on me.

No jealous pang shall mar my pure affection;
    For while 'tis true your heart I'm forced to share
With that French doll with pink and white complexion,
    The Pussy Cat, the Lamb and Teddy Bear,
'Tis mine alone, whate'er the time or place is,
    To know your every grief and each delight;
I feel your childish wrath and warm embraces,
    I share your little pillow every night.
And so, without another why or whether
    I'll love you while my stitches hold together.

ARTHUR GUITERMAN

MONA

(*a little gipsy girl speaks*)

A lady came right to our tent
To have her fortune told.
A little girl was with her,
Well just about as old
As I am. And she had such lovely
Pretty clothes and things,
A pocketbook, such dainty socks,
But not as many rings
As I have. And she hadn't ear rings
Either — just like me.

She seemed to be all fluffed and fussed
And nice as she could be.
Her shoes were tight I know they were.
My feet are always bare.
Her hat was tight and hot,
I let the breeze blow through my hair.
She sat so still and stiff and prim
Upon my Nana's chair.
She smiled just once. I skinned the cat
Three times to make her stare.

And later on she whispered
That her name was Gwendolyn.
But I'd rather just be me
And dance to Toto's Mandolin.

GRETTA M. MC OMBER

TWO LITTLE SHADOWS

(*to introduce a minuet*)

Two little shadows soft as smoke
Come to my house to play.
Two little frisky shadow folk
Follow me round the day.
And whether they're shod with fairy shoon
I have never noticed yet;
But one little shadow's a Pantaloon
And one is a Pantalette.

Out of a bundle of rusty rhymes,
Off of a page perchance,
Two little shadows oftentimes
Come to my door to dance.
Under the willows they silhouette
And silver the afternoon
And one little shadow's a Pantalette
And one is a Pantaloon.

Two little shadows soft as smoke
Knock at my door and wait —
Two little frisky shadow folk
Swing on my creakety gate.
And whether they slid from a sliver of moon
Or out of a dream I forget,
But one little shadow's a Pantaloon
And one is a Pantalette.

MILDRED PLEW MERRYMAN

THOUGHTS OF A LONG–LEGGED FRENCH DOLL

Some folks think I'm a moron dumb,
   Because of my hair I suppose.
I'm really discreet; a wise doll keeps
   And never reveals all she knows.

But the things I see, O mercy me,
   They'd fill a book and more.
They make my stuffing lumpy with glee
   With stitches my side seams grow sore.

What do I ponder on, sitting here?
   On feet, and hands, and eyes.
Why do they move in motion queer?
   They fill me with surprise.

I sit all day quite motionless,
   And never blink a lash.
I must confess I'm notionless,
   Why do folks act so rash?

Why do folks say the things they do,
   Raving on more and more?
Don't they know that's foolish too?
   It's all been said before!

And why is this day Saturday?
   Who told you it was so?
Why don't you call it Whateverday?
   And where did the yesterdays go?

What makes everyone laugh so loud?
   What do they mean by fun?
What seems like wit to a jovial crowd
   Might bore another one.

Why do people laugh at me?
      They're as funny as I.
I'll keep my arms about my knee
      And let the world go by.

AUDREY F. CARPENTER

❖ ❖ ❖

SUPERSTITION

O dearie me! Ise all upsot an' feelin' kinda blue,
Ise in an awful 'dickerment an' don' know what to do.
Wuz feelin' mighty lonesome an' ah axed de Lawd to send
A little baby down to me so ah could hev a friend.
Ah didn't say what color, didn't speechify de kind
'Cause Mammy says de good Lawd knows jes' what is in
      yo' mind.
He lubs to gib what yo' expect an' sometimes eben mo'!
Dat's true — ah on'y axed fo' one; de Lawd done sent me fo'.

Fo' little baby pussy cats an' one ob dem is white.
De oder free am awful dark; dey's mos' as black as night.
My Pappy looked dem ober in a 'stitious sort o' way
An' say us wont be lucky if dem black ones gwine to stay.
Den Mammy looked at Pappy an' she say, " Now see here
      Buck,
How offen mus' ah tell yo' dat dey's no sich thing as luck.
Yo life am what you make it an' ah shouldn't be s'prised
Ef dem dar baby kittens wasn't blessin's in disguise."

Dey bofe is argufyin' kase my Pappy is no saint.
Mammy says ise gwine to keep dem an' Pappy says ah aint.
She say my Pappy sho am wrong an' 'stitiousness am sin.
Ah think my Mammy mus' be right, ah hopes she's gwine
      to win.

Ah feels my 'sponsibility; it makes me kinda blue.
Ah lubs dem free black babies an' ah knows dey lubs me too.
But if ah has to part wid dem when dis yer fuss am done
Ah hopes de Lawd jes' members dat ah on'y axed fer one.

JAMES W. STANISTREET

❖ ❖ ❖

IN THE DAYS OF LAFAYETTE

Here in this corner of the stair,
A portrait hangs, of a girl so fair
That one's glances cling to the lovely eyes,
That look with an innocent surprise
Out of the gloomy canvas there;
Low-necked gown and powdered hair,
That was grandmamma's self, my dear.
Out of the gloom — ah, long ago —
Her sweet face shone; and down the stair
Slender and graceful, tall and fair,
Grandma came, with footstep light,
To go to the general's ball one night.
With throbbing heart and flashing eyes,
She entered the ball-room, large and grand,
Lights are gleaming on every hand —
Rustle of silk and shimmer of lace,
Delicate laughter and youth and grace,
Music that throbs on the heavy air,
That sobs and dies; that leaps again
Into new life, with a clearer strain,
As the dancers form for the minuet,
Led by the gallant Lafayette.
Whom for his partner would he choose!
He, the honored and loved of all —
Beauty and wealth, in the brilliant hall,

Maid and madam waited to see
If she the general's choice might be —
But haughty grand dames, he passed them by.
His eyes were fixed on a dainty face
Full of a tender, nameless grace,
The face of a girl with shining eyes,
And lo! at her feet, on bended knee
'Tis he, the honored of all the land,
Asking gently for her hand,
Begging the favor granted be
From the little maid who blushed to see.
Proud little figure, he led her out,
And down from above the music came,
Leaped on the air from its sheath of flame,
Leaped into exquisite melody,
As step by step, ah, grave and slow
Back and forth and to and fro,
Bending low with hand on heart,
The stately dancers meet and part.
Dear little maid, with rose-leaf face,
Gliding slowly to her place;
Bending, turning, curtseying low,
Drooping upon bended knee
To her gallant vis-a-vis,
She told her heart in that fairy glow
That should she live to be old, so old,
Never oh never would she forget
That she danced with the General Lafayette.
Over her hand he bent his head
" To the fairest," were the words he said,
Bidding adieu to the little maid;
The rose she gave and the hand as well
Are dust these many, many years —
The only things that do not die
Are memories, dear, and memory's tears.

Grandmamma, in your quaint old gown,
Out of your oval frame step down,
Lead us with your statelier tread
And gentle hand, to the days long dead,
Back to the night you can't forget,
When you danced with our hero — Lafayette.

GRACE MARLIN RAINES

❖ ❖ ❖

PIRATES

Oh I wish I were a pirate
A bloody, thirsty, pirate,
A happy jolly pirate,
On the deep blue sea.

Oh if I were a pirate,
I'd paint my face all red,
And hold a knife between my teeth,
And never go to bed.

I'd scour all the seas,
My men would think me bold,
And I would steal from haughty kings
Their daughters, young and old.

I'd sail around with pirate men,
In a pirate's gay attire,
And we would cross through ocean waves,
Like roaring, soaring, fire.

But though my outward self seemed bold
At heart I would be kind,
And any man both brave and true,
Could be a friend of mine.

[268]

Oh I'd love to be a pirate,
A wild and naughty pirate,
A bad but goodly pirate,
On a storming, dashing sea.

HENRIETTA SEARLE MOONEY (14 years)

❖ ❖ ❖

GOLF

You find the links and make a " tee "
Then place the ball there as you see
And hit it hard as hard can be,
      That's golf.

You miss the ball and hit your toe
And then you say the Scotch for " Oh "
It's all part of the game you know
      It's golf.

You stop a ball next with your eye
They call out " Fore " you wonder why;
Up mounts your score, although you try —
      That's golf.

You get wet through and dismally
Crawl home to get a different tea
But on the links next morn you'll be —
      That's Golf.

❖ ❖ ❖

CICELY CROAK

In the little hamlet of Daisyoak
There lived a maiden named Cicely Croak,
As bright and comely a country lass
As ever peeped into a looking-glass;

But life with Cicely seemed askew,
For her favorite color was indigo blue;
And true to her name, she would croak and croak,
Till it came to pass as a family joke
That Cicely'd push the world downhill,
And tumble after it, croaking still.
If the weather were cold, she knew she should freeze,
And she'd wrap her in furs from her head to her knees.
If the weather were hot, 'twas going to be hotter,
And they all would perish for lack of water;
And a cloud in the west would surely bring
A thunder-storm, cyclone, or some such thing;
If the baby'd a pain or the father an ache,
Pretty Cicely's curls would go shakety-shake,
And she'd prophesy death, and arouse their fears,
Till brothers and sisters were all in tears.
And thus said the people of Daisyoak,
" True to her name is Cicely Croak."

One fine June morning it befell
That good Mrs. Croak had eggs to sell;
So Cicely, donning her dark blue gown,
Set off on the road to Barleytown —
To Barleytown, with its walls and spires,
Its market-place, and its crowds of buyers.
Oh, Barleytown on a market-day
Was the place where Cicely loved to stay.
But miles of woodland lay between
Fair Barleytown and these hills of green,
And Cicely thought, with a little shiver,
Of the lonely road by the winding river,
And the grewsome forest just at hand,
Whose depths might shelter a robber band.
A robber band! and her heart beat fast
As rabbit or squirrel darted past;

A robber band! and Cicely Croak
Wished she were home in Daisyoak.
She had often traversed this self same way,
But ever before till this very day
The weather had met her mind's demands,
And she'd never bethought her of robber bands.
And now it was neither too hot nor too cold,
And the sunshine flooded the land with gold;
Not a cloud was afloat in the clear blue sky,
And the breeze was sweet as it drifted by.
At length, through the stillness, Cicely heard
A sound that was neither of beast nor bird —
A lightsome whistle — and swift she scanned
The road and the fields on either hand;
But no living thing could she espy,
Save a startled wren and a butterfly.
Still louder and louder the whistling grew.
Then, rounding a corner, came in view
A youth in a broad-brimmed steeple hat,
Leading a heifer sleek and fat —
A handsome youth in a suit of gray,
With a bright red rose, befitting the day.
Thought Cicely — " Only a farmer's son.
How glad I am that I did not run! "
Then she stole sly glances up and down
The folds and frills of her dark blue gown,
And she thought to herself, with a flush of red,
" We shall meet at the cross-roads just ahead."

The whistling ceased. " A right merry day,"
Said the stranger youth in the suit of gray;
And Cicely courtesied with maidenly grace,
While she noted the honest, cheery face,
The bright knee-buckles and silken hose,
The pointed hat and the red, red rose.

"My name," said the youth, "is Hilary Hope;
I come from the village of Silverslope
To sell my heifer at Barleytown,
And to buy my mother a new silk gown.
So if, fair maiden, you go my way,
You will let me walk beside, I pray;
For two on a lonely road," quoth he,
"Are better than one, as you'll agree."
Then Cicely dimpled and drooped her head.
"I am glad of your company, sir," she said;
" 'Tis always stupid to walk alone,
And two are better than one, I own."
And thus they came into Barleytown,
The pointed hat and the dark blue gown.

The eggs and the heifer were quickly sold
For goodly prices in shining gold,
And Cicely helped to choose the silk,
And the beautiful lace as white as milk,
That were bought by the loving Hilary Hope
For the dear old mother in Silverslope;
And they looked at this and they talked of that,
And they laughed at the tricks of a showman's cat,
And they ate their luncheon of cake and cheese
Under the spreading chestnut-trees,
And Cicely's heart was as light as her toes,
And she wore on her bosom a cream-white rose.

As the days sped onward, all the folk
Listened in vain for Cicely's croak.
The wind might howl and the rain might pour,
But Cicely only would laugh the more,
With never a frown to mar the grace
Of the joyous brow and the winsome face;

And father and mother, wondering, smiled,
Saying, " What can have come over the child? "
And the children, talking among themselves,
Said that a charm had been wrought by the elves —
Those curious creatures, wrinkled and brown,
Who lived in the forest of Barleytown.
And Cicely heard, but she did not say
How she came to see 'twas the happier way
To be cheery and brave, and to hope for the best,
Than to croak and fear and be ever distressed.
So onward the moments merrily rolled,
Whether the skies were gray or gold.

A wedding followed, all in good time,
With a feast, a dance, and a nuptial rhyme,
And Cicely's heart was as light as her toes,
And she wore on her bosom a cream-white rose.
And thus say the people of Silverslope,
" True to her name is Cicely Hope."

EMMA C. DOWD

❖ ❖ ❖

GRANDMOTHER'S STORY OF BUNKER HILL BATTLE

(as she saw it from the belfry June 17, 1775)

'Tis like stirring living embers when, at eighty, one remembers
All the achings and the quakings of " the times that tried
men's souls; "
When I talk of WHIG and TORY, when I tell the REBEL
story,
To you the words are ashes, but to me they're burning coals.

I had heard the muskets' rattle of the April running battle;
Lord Percy's hunted soldiers, I can see their red coats still;
But a deadly chill comes o'er me, as the day looms up before me,
When a thousand men lay bleeding on the slopes of Bunker's Hill.

'Twas a peaceful summer's morning, when the first thing gave us warning
Was the booming of the cannon from the river and the shore:
" Child," says grandma, " what's the matter, what is all this noise and clatter?
Have those scalping Indian devils come to murder us once more? "

Poor old soul! my sides were shaking in the midst of all my quaking
To hear her talk of Indians when the guns began to roar:
She had seen the burning village, and the slaughter and the pillage,
When the Mohawks killed her father, with their bullets through his door.

Then I said, " Now, dear old granny, don't you fret and worry any,
For I'll soon come back and tell you whether this is work or play;
There can't be mischief in it, so I won't be gone a minute — "
For a minute then I started. I was gone the livelong day.

No time for bodice-lacing or for looking-glass grimacing;
Down my hair went as I hurried, tumbling half-way to my heels;

God forbid your ever knowing, when there's blood around
    her flowing,
How the lonely, helpless daughter of a quiet household feels!

In the street I heard a thumping; and I knew it was the
    stumping
Of the Corporal, our old neighbor, on the wooden leg he
    wore,
With a knot of women round him, — it was lucky I had
    found him, —
So I followed with the others, and the Corporal marched
    before.

They were making for the steeple, — the old soldier and his
    people;
The pigeons circled round us as we climbed the creaking
    stair,
Just across the narrow river — O, so close it made me
    shiver! —
Stood a fortress on the hilltop that but yesterday was bare.

Not slow our eyes to find it; well we knew who stood be-
    hind it,
Though the earthwork hid them from us, and the stubborn
    walls were dumb:
Here were sister, wife, and mother, looking wild upon each
    other,
And their lips were white with terror as they said, THE
    HOUR HAS COME!

The morning slowly wasted, not a morsel had we tasted,
And our heads were almost splitting with the cannons'
    deafening thrill,

When a figure tall and stately round the rampart strode
  sedately;
It was PRESCOTT, one since told me; he commanded on
  the hill.

Every woman's heart grew bigger when we saw his manly
  figure,
With the banyan buckled round it, standing up so straight
  and tall;
Like a gentleman of leisure who is strolling out for pleasure,
Through the storm of shells and cannon-shot he walked
  around the wall.

At eleven the streets were swarming, for the red-coats' ranks
  were forming;
At noon in marching order they were moving to the piers;
How the bayonets gleamed and glistened, as we looked far
  down and listened
To the trampling and the drum-beat of the belted grena-
  diers!

At length the men have started, with a cheer (it seemed
  fainthearted),
In their scarlet regimentals, with their knapsacks on their
  backs,
And the reddening, rippling water, as after a sea-fight's
  slaughter,
Round the barges gliding onward blushed like blood along
  their tracks.

So they crossed to the other border, and again they formed
  in order;
And the boats came back for soldiers, came for soldiers,
  soldiers still:

The time seemed everlasting to us women faint and fast-
  ing, —
At last they're moving, marching, marching proudly up the
  hill.

We can see the bright steel glancing all along the lines
  advancing —
Now the front rank fires a volley — they have thrown away
  their shot;
For behind the earthwork lying, all the balls above them
  flying,
Our people need not hurry; so they wait and answer not.

Then the Corporal, our old cripple (he would swear sometimes and tipple), —
He had heard the bullets whistle (in the old French war)
  before, —
Calls out in words of jeering, just as if they all were
  hearing, —
And his wooden leg thumps fiercely on the dusty belfry
  floor: —

" Oh! fire away, ye villians, and earn King George's shillin's,
But ye'll waste a ton of powder afore a ' rebel ' falls;
You may bang the dirt and welcome, they're as safe as
  Dan'l Malcolm
Ten foot beneath the gravestone that you've splintered with
  your balls! "

In the hush of expectation, in the awe and trepidation
Of the dread approaching moment, we are well-nigh breathing all;
Though the rotten bars are falling on the rickety belfry
  railing,
We are crowding up against them like the waves against a
  wall.

Just a glimpse (the air is clearer), they are nearer, — nearer, — nearer,
When a flash — a curling smoke-wreath — then a crash — the steeple shakes —
The deadly truce is ended; the tempest's shroud is rended;
Like a morning mist it gathered, like a thunder-cloud it breaks!

O the sight our eyes discover as the blue-black smoke blows over!
The red-coats stretched in windrows as a mower rakes his hay;
Here a scarlet heap is lying, there a headlong crowd is flying
Like a billow that has broken and is shivered into spray.

Then we cried, " The troops are routed! they are beat — it can't be doubted!
God be thanked, the fight is over! " — Ah! the grim old soldier's smile!
" Tell us, tell us why you look so? " (we could hardly speak, we shook so), —
" Are they beaten? ARE they beaten? *ARE* they beaten? " — " Wait a while."

O the trembling and the terror! for too soon we saw our error:
They are baffled, not defeated; we have driven them back in vain;
And the columns that were scattered, round the colors that were tattered,
Toward the sullen silent fortress turn their belted breasts again.

[278]

All at once, as we are gazing, lo the roofs of Charlestown
    blazing!
They have fired the harmless village; in an hour it will be
    down!
The Lord in heaven confound them, rain his fire and brim-
    stone round them, —
The robbing, murdering red-coats, that would burn a peace-
    ful town!

They are marching, stern and solemn; we can see each
    massive column
As they near the naked earth-mound with the slanting walls
    so steep.
Have our soldiers got faint-hearted, and in noiseless haste
    departed?
Are they panic-struck and helpless?   Are they palsied or
    asleep?

Now! the walls they're almost under! scarce a rod the foes
    asunder!
Not a firelock flashed against them! up the earthwork they
    will swarm!
But the words have scarce been spoken, when the ominous
    calm is broken,
And a bellowing crash has emptied all the vengeance of the
    storm!

So again, with murderous slaughter, pelted backward to the
    water,
Fly Pigot's running heroes and the frightened braves of
    Howe;
And we shout, "At last they're done for, it's their barges
    they have run for:
They are beaten, beaten, beaten; and the battle's over
    now!"

And we looked, poor timid creatures, on the rough old
    soldier's features,
Our lips afraid to question, but he knew what we would
    ask;
"Not sure," he said; "keep quiet, — once more, I guess,
    they'll try it —
Here's a damnation to the cut-throats! " — then he handed
    me his flask,

Saying, " Gal, you're looking shaky; have a drop of old
    Jamaiky:
I'm afraid there'll be more trouble afore this job is done; "
So I took one scorching swallow; dreadful faint I felt and
    hollow,
Standing there from early morning when the firing was
    begun.

All through those hours of trial I had watched a calm clock
    dial,
As the hands kept creeping, creeping, — they were creeping
    round to four,
When the old man said, " They're forming with their bayo-
    nets fixed for storming:
It's the death grip that's a coming, — they will try the works
    once more."

With brazen trumphets blaring, the flames behind them
    glaring,
The deadly wall before them, in a close array they come;
Still onward, upward toiling, like a dragon's fold uncoiling —
Like the rattlesnake's shrill warning the reverberating drum!
Over heaps all torn and gory — shall I tell the fearful story,
How they surged above the breastwork, as a sea breaks over
    a deck;

How, driven, yet scarce defeated, our worn-out men retreated,
With their powder-horns all emptied, like the swimmers
from a wreck?

It has all been told and painted; as for me, they say I
fainted,
And the wooden-legged old Corporal stumped with me down
the stair:
When I woke from dreams affrighted the evening lamps were
lighted, —
On the floor a youth was lying; his bleeding breast was
bare.

And I heard through all the flurry, " Send for WARREN!
hurry! hurry!
Tell him here's a soldier bleeding, and he'll come and dress
his wound! "
Ah, we knew not till the morrow told its tale of death and
sorrow,
How the starlight found him stiffened on the dark and
bloody ground.

Who the youth was, what his name was, where the place
from which he came was,
Who had brought him from the battle, and had left him
at our door,
He could not speak to tell us; but 'twas one of our brave
fellows,
As the homespun plainly showed us which the dying soldier
wore.

For they all thought he was dying, as they gathered 'round
him crying, —
And they said, " O, how they'll miss him! " and, " What will
his mother do? "

Then, his eyelids just unclosing like a child's that has been
    dozing,
He faintly murmured, " Mother! " —— and — I saw his
    eyes were blue.

— " Why, grandma, how you're winking! " — Ah, my child,
    it sets me thinking
Of a story not like this one. Well, he somehow lived along;
So we came to know each other, and I nursed him like a —
    mother,
Till at last he stood before me, tall, and rosy-cheeked, and
    strong.

And we sometimes walked together in the pleasant summer
    weather;
— " Please to tell us what his name was? " — Just your
    own, my little dear, —
There's his picture Copley painted: we became so well ac-
    quainted,
That — in short, that's why I'm grandma, and you children
    all are here!

OLIVER WENDELL HOLMES

❖ ❖ ❖

ROBIN GOODFELLOW

From Oberon, in fairy land,
   The king of ghosts and shadows there,
Mad Robin I, at his command,
   Am sent to view the night-sports here.
     What revel rout
     Is kept about,
   In every corner where I go,
     I will o'ersee,
     And merry be,
   And make good sport, with ho, ho, ho!

More swift than lightning can I fly
  About this airy welkin soon,
And in a minute's space, descry
  Each thing that's done below the moon.
      There's not a hag
      Or ghost shall wag,
  Or cry, 'ware goblins! where I go;
      But Robin I
      Their feats will spy,
  And send them home with ho, ho, ho!

Whene'er such wanderers I meet,
  As from their night-sports they trudge home,
With counterfeiting voice I greet,
  And call them on with me to roam;
      Through woods, through lakes;
      Through bogs, through brakes;
  Or else, unseen, with them I go.
      All in the nick
      To play some trick,
  And frolic it, with ho, ho, ho!

Sometimes I meet them like a man,
  Sometimes an ox, sometimes a hound;
And to a horse I turn me can,
  To trip and trot about them round.
      But if to ride
      My back they stride,
  More swift than wind away I go,
      O'er hedge and lands,
      Through pools and ponds,
  I hurry, laughing, ho, ho, ho!

Yet now and then, the maids to please,
  At midnight I card up their wool;
And, while they sleep and take their ease,
  With wheel to threads their flax I pull.
    I grind at mill
    Their malt up still;
  I dress their hemp; I spin their tow;
    If any wake,
    And would me take,
  I wend me, laughing ho, ho, ho!

From hag-bred Merlin's time, have I
  Thus nightly revel'd to and fro;
And for my pranks men call me by
  The name of Robin Goodfellow.
    Fiends, ghosts, sprites,
    Who haunt the nights,
  The hags and goblins do me know;
    And beldames old
    My feats have told,
  So Vale, vale; ho, ho, ho!

BEN JONSON

❖ ❖ ❖

PIERROT

(to precede a dance)

Once, just once in the month of June,
  When the moon is full and low,
Out of the shadows' soft cocoon,
  Capering to and fro,

Back through the leafy lanes he comes,
  Clown of the long ago,
  While the beetle hums
  And the cricket strums,
    " Pierrot!
      Pierrot!
      Pierrot! "

White as the moths that drift and drown,
  White as the petal snow,
Treading a musty moonbeam down,
  Twirling a tricksy toe,
Back he comes on capering feet,
  Clown of the long ago,
  While the bat wings beat
  And the owls repeat,
    " Pierrot!
      Pierrot!
      Pierrot! "

Once, just once in a musty moon,
  When the pink wild roses blow,
Back through the leafy lanes of June,
  Lanes that he used to know,
Out of the painted past he comes,
  Capering to and fro,
  While the beetle hums
  And the cricket strums,
    " Pierrot!
      Pierrot!
      Pierrot! "

                    MILDRED PLEW MERRYMAN

THE CEDAR CHEST

There are lots of pleasant things to do on a dark and
  rainy day;
But Sister and I like best of all to go in the garret and
  play.
There are trunks and boxes and bundles there, old chairs
  and a couch or so,
And many a bunch of drying herbs hung up in a fragrant
  row.
And hidden away in the fartherest nook is the queer old
  cedar chest
Where Grandmother carefully stores away the treasures
  she loves the best.
Quaint old gowns with flowery sprigs smelling of lavender,
Satin and chintz and bombazine, figured brocade and fan.
Odd little shoes with ribbons worn, mittens of strange design
A wee parasol of watered silk and a billowing crinoline.
There's an ostrich plume and an ivory fan
And a cloak of brown homespun,
We try them all on, Sister and I, and we have lots of fun.
I like to fasten my curls up high and dress in this flowered
  gown
And wear this sweet little pancake hat and go walking up
  and down.
I feel like a lady of long ago and my mother smiles at me
And says I look like a fashion plate of 1863.
But when Sister wears the crinoline and walks down stairs
  just so
Grandmother says, "Why you look like me, seventy years
  ago!"

EDITH OSBORNE

The king is in the counting house counting out his money.
The clock strikes twelve and in he comes
Demanding bread and honey.
The queen is in the garden hanging out the clothes
The king he calls and he calls again
But the queen holds high her nose.
Now like Jack Sprat the king likes fat;
The queen she likes the lean,
And so on menus they wouldn't agree.
The king pushes back his cup of tea
And leaves the dining room, flat.
He wanders out along the road
All hungry and despairing.
Along comes Peter the Pumpkin Eater —
On a pony he comes tearing.
The king he stops the happy man
And asks him, " Why so jolly? "
And Peter says, " My lord I can
If only you will folly."
The king he reaches up his ear,
And this is what he hears:
" Peter Peter Pumpkin Eater
Had a wife and couldn't keep her;
I put her in a pumpkin shell
And now I keep her very well."
Just then Little Miss Muffet who'd sat on a tuffet
Came screaming, " A spider, a spider! "
And the king's first thought it was of course,
" To hide her, yes, to hide her."
And quickly then he sits him down,
Himself upon her skirts.
Spider comes by and never sees —
Panting and running in spurts.
Little Miss Muffet so grateful is she

Has nothing to offer but whey.
However the king so famished is he
Drinks it off in a draught and is gay.
And now the king of whom we sing
Has little to worry him left
He's only to find him a grand pumpking —
When startled is he by the news of a theft.
Tom Tom the Piper's son
Stole a pig and away he run.
The king cries out, " He must be caught,"
And called for his grand armee.
And still his shouting comes to naught,
For all the king's horses and all the king's men
Were putting Humpty Dumpty together again.
Defeated again our monarch is sad,
Then wearily goes on his way
Till Little Jack Horner who never is bad
Comes out of his corner to say his say —
The king's eyes glitter when he sees that pie,
" Oh give me a piece or I'll surely die."
And Little Jack Horner to prove his worth
Gives enough pie to increase the king's girth.
Now once again the king is glad
But see, a maiden in distress.
With half an eye our hero sees that she's in bad.
" I'm little Bo Peep; I've lost my sheep
And don't know where to find them."
The king replies (he loves to advise)
" Let them alone and they'll come home
Wagging their tails behind them."
The Knave of Hearts, you know him well,
He bumps into the king pelmel.
The king, he sees the fancy tarts
And well he knows the queen's fine art.
He seizes the rascal by the throat

And drags him back across the moat.
The queen whom we left with her nose in the air
Is now deep down in the depths of despair.
She'd made those tarts to please the king
And now, oh now, how can she sing?
When what to her wondering eyes should appear
But his majesty dragging the knave by an ear.
The Queen's so happy to see the king;
The king's so thrilled with everything —
The tarts, the knave are all forgot
In joyful pleasure at their lot.
The cat's crept in
But then who cares?
Even a cat may look at a king.

Now let us sing
Long live the king!
The queen, oh long live she!
And if they ever quarrel again
May we be there to see.

GRACE MARIE STANISTREET

❖ ❖ ❖

A FAREWELL

My fairest child, I have no song to give you,
No lark could pipe in skies so dull and gray,
Yet if you will, one quiet hint I'll leave you
    For every day.

I'll tell you how to sing a clearer carol
Than lark who hails the dawn or breezy down,
To earn yourself a purer poets laurel
    Than Shakespeare's crown.

Be good sweet maid, and let who can be clever.
Do lovely things, not dream them all day long,
And so make Life, Death and that vast Forever
One grand sweet song.

CHARLES KINGSLEY